Will It Stand Up?

A Professional Engineer's View of the Creation of the
London 2012 Olympic Stadium

Derek Allen Mason

Dear Neil and Karen
    Here is a copy of my book as a
thank you for your support over the
years. I hope you enjoy reading it.

    Best Regards   Derek

RETHINK PRESS

First published in Great Britain 2017
by Rethink Press (www.rethinkpress.com)

This book is dedicated to all those people who were told that they could not do something, but held onto their dreams and proved that they could do it, as I have done many times in my life and career.

PRAISE FOR *WILL IT STAND UP?*

Derek Mason is a highly respected and successful engineer and businessman who writes with experience and authority about the Olympic stadium project in which he was intimately involved. The stadium was a business as well as an aesthetic success and this book helpfully draws out the broader lessons which others can learn from.

Rt Hon Sir Vince Cable

'Will It Stand Up?' is a unique insight into the technical prowess and in-depth technical intelligence that goes on behind the scenes of large construction projects such as the Olympic Stadium. Many of the processes Derek discusses are transferable to smaller projects and business and will be useful for switched-on managers to help guide them.

Jez Rose, behaviourist, broadcaster and award-winning author

Derek is a structural engineer who thinks like a marketer. This book is so darned useful because the seven principles that Derek describes so eloquently will make the execution and implementation of any project more successful. It's a great story, well told and with some bloody useful take-aways.

Nigel Botterill – Founder of the Entrepreneur's Circle and award-winning author

In 'Will It Stand Up?', Derek describes the seven principles to running a successful project that I have seen him apply throughout his career in projects of various sizes and complexities with great success. At the heart of all seven principles, and the key to achieving them, is good communication. Without good communication you probably won't even get to agree the first principle. However, focus on the communication and, as this book shows, the seven principles work when applied to projects from small domestic ones to projects in excess of £50 million. This book will help the reader understand these seven principles and how to apply them to their projects to achieve the success they desire.

Ritchie Clapson CEngMIStructE – former Managing Director, Capita Bobrowski

CONTENTS

Introduction

Welcome to Will It Stand Up?

This book has been written for architects, structural engineers, developers and contractors and anyone interested in construction projects, especially sports stadiums and other major leisure facilities. It also applies to smaller projects, such as residential or commercial projects.

Will It Stand Up? is a blueprint for building your personal and business reputation. In this book, I introduce the seven principles of running a successful project. I explain and illustrate them by using the London 2012 Olympic stadium as an example of how they were applied successfully. There are also examples of other construction projects where I have followed these principles.

The structure of this book

Will It Stand Up? tracks the journey of creating the London 2012 Olympic stadium from the beginning. Starting with the initial bid, it moves on to the planning and designing, through the detailed design and construction, right up to the opening and closing ceremonies. It shows how this was done and highlights lessons learned that helped make the project a success. It tells the story of an Olympic stadium with the largest ever number of demountable elements, which would enable the 80,000-seat stadium to be converted into a stadium with 25,000 permanent seats after the Games. This had never been attempted before London 2012.

With this focus on temporary elements, London 2012 represented a new era for Olympic stadium design. It combined the high-level performance needed for a major sports event with the long-term needs of the community. This was crucial so that the stadium met the legacy requirements and did not become a white elephant.

The biggest problems of projects of this size and complexity are communication and ensuring that every member of the team knows what they are meant to do and by when. This has to be monitored so that everyone stays on track and the various milestones are met. The collaboration that was required to interpret the client's brief and architectural design and translate this into the structural solution that was finally chosen and built will be discussed in detail, using examples.

You will gain insights into how the project was completed successfully and find ways to use the lessons learned in your own projects. Each chapter describes one of the seven principles and looks at how that principle will benefit your business. Using the London 2012 Olympic stadium as the model, we look at how each principle was applied during the design and build.

The recipe for success and the lessons learned are summarised at the end of each section, so you can refer to them and apply them to your own projects.

Background

I am passionate about engineering and athletics. I've been a professional structural engineer for more than thirty years and I've had a successful athletics career for more than forty years. I wanted to combine my passion for both of these by writing a useful book for my fellow professionals in the construction industry.

I led the team that did the third-party check of the structural design of the London 2012 Olympic stadium and I'm very proud of the part that I played in its success. I wanted to use this excellent project as the background to this book to show why it was such a successful project for London, the UK and the Olympic Games.

The seven principles of running a successful project emerged from my personal observations of the methods that Team Stadium used to build an outstanding stadium, within time and budget. I realised that these methods reflected the values that I have always held and that have helped me build my own successful structural engineering practice.

Will It Stand Up? brings together all my experience into a helpful blueprint for those who want to take their construction project or design company to a higher level.

My story

I was born to British parents in a suburb of Cape Town in South Africa in 1963. I was the second eldest of four children, with my brother being one year older than me. Like many young boys, my brother and I used to do a lot of things together. We were always trying to build things and I remember us saving our pocket money to buy nails and hammers to make things out of wood. This is where my interest in engineering and construction started: I was always interested in how things were put together and made.

At secondary school, I discovered I had an aptitude for maths and science, and this formed a good grounding for my future engineering career. It was in my first year of secondary school, when I was 13 years' old, that my athletics career really started, although it nearly ended before it began. This was more than forty years ago, and coaching in the middle-distance events was not what it is today.

The first day I met my athletics coach, he looked me up and down and asked me if I'd come to waste his time. I did not look like an athlete, and definitely not a middle-distance athlete, according to him. Naturally, I was rather shocked, but I had a choice: I could believe him and just leave and forget about running middle distances, or I could show him that he was wrong.

I was a typical teenager of that age. Things were hard financially at home and I had had a tough upbringing, so I had developed a strong will. Therefore, I decided to show the coach that he was wrong in his assessment of me. I decided to learn as much as I could about athletics and to train as hard as possible to be the best that I could be.

My childhood athletics heroes were Sebastian Coe and Steve Ovett. As part of my learning about athletics, and the training aspects in particular, I came across various books. One of these was *Winning Running* by Sebastian's father, Peter Coe, on the methods that he used for training Sebastian. I followed Seb Coe's athletic career and was inspired by his achievements and battles with Steve Ovett. Not only were they fellow countrymen but they ended up breaking each other's world records, sometimes within a few weeks of one of them setting a new record.

While I did not possess the natural talent of Seb Coe or Steve Ovett, I decided I would make the coach take notice by becoming the best that I could be. I did this through dedicated training and by improving my knowledge of athletics and training methods. I trained twice a day, sometimes even three times a day, to make sure I was fulfilling my potential. Within two years I'd become the school champion in the 800 metres, 1,500 metres and 3,000 metres, all in record times.

In the next two years, I achieved the same in the higher age group, also holding school open records for these distances and achieving Provincial B Colours for the 1,500-metre steeplechase. This shows what you can do with dedicated training, application and a strong will.

In the winter months, I ran cross-country to keep fit and build my strength and stamina. I then progressed to road races, including 5-, 10- and 15-kilometre events and half-marathons. I ran my first marathon aged 18 when I was in the army doing my two years of conscripted service. I only had four days of running training, but I still finished in a respectable 3 hours and 25 minutes.

I've now been running seriously for more than forty years and have completed about sixty half-marathons and more than a hundred full marathons, and thirteen 35-mile ultramarathons.

After completing my two years of national service as an infantry corporal, I enrolled in a technical college for my engineering studies, as I could not afford to go to university. After that I went to work for a company full time, but because I didn't have a degree I wasn't allowed to do design work. I then won a bursary and entered the third year of the BSc civil engineering course at the University of Cape Town before progressing to my master's degree in civil engineering at the same university, which I received in 1992.

I then worked for various companies in Africa before coming to London in 1998. It was here that I had the opportunity to manage the team that carried out the engineering and technical review of the London 2012 Olympic stadium, which was the highlight of my engineering career at that stage.

I learned through running that dedication and hard work do pay off, especially if they are combined with intelligent training and application. To be successful you have to put into practice what you learn, and I do this with my engineering and business. I enjoy the variety of structural engineering work, using my experience and knowledge to solve problems in a way that makes a difference to people's lives and helps them realise their dreams.

How to use this book

Will It Stand Up? gives examples of how the seven principles of running a successful project were applied to the London 2012 Olympic stadium and explains how you can use them in other projects.

The seven principles of running a successful project are:

1 Have a common goal

2 Develop a good detailed plan before you start

3 Develop a good communication strategy

4 Develop the ethos of good teamwork

5 Decide on the legacy from the outset

6 Develop robust checking procedures before you start

7 Make sure your project is fit for purpose.

I hope that when you apply these principles in your business they will have the same impact as they have had on my career, bringing you more repeat business and more word-of-mouth referrals, enhancing your business reputation and building your financial and professional success.

CHAPTER 1
THE COMMON GOAL

The International Olympic Committee has the honour of announcing that the Games of the XXX Olympiad are awarded to the city of London.

Jacques Rogge, President of the International Olympic Committee

The bid for the 2012 Olympics

These twenty-three words spoken by Jacques Rogge, President of the International Olympic Committee (IOC), announced to the world that the 2012 Olympic Games had been awarded to the city of London. It had been a long process, but the UK Bid Team had a common goal of creating a lasting legacy for future generations and a desire to inspire young people all over the world. It was this vision that made them determined to win.

This chapter details the process that the UK Bid Team followed to win the 2012 Olympics for London and the UK, and the first steps taken to move this massive project forward. It focuses on why it is important to have a single common goal and how this enabled the team to win and host what became the most successful Games in modern Olympic history.

The importance of a common goal

Just as in the UK Olympic bid, having a common goal is the first principle of effectively managing any construction project. It is central to the successful design and completion of your project.

PRINCIPLE 1: HAVE A COMMON GOAL

If the team does not have a common goal, the individual team members will concentrate on what they think is important and the team's efforts will be diluted. This can waste time and money, as resources are not used effectively. Having a common goal creates team spirit, encouraging everyone to contribute and work together towards a shared vision, whatever their role.

If the team is united in a common goal, each member of the team will consider that the team's work is likely to achieve an outcome that is greater than their own contribution. In other words, a united team with a common purpose will achieve a result that is greater than the sum of the individual contributions made.

A common goal will do the following:

- Give the team and individual members a sense of purpose.

- Keep each individual and the whole team focused on what the team wants to achieve.

- Give each team member a method of solving a problem, dealing with a situation or developing part of the work, measured against a set of well-defined goals and objectives. This will ensure that the solution meets the objectives of the project.

- Give discipline to the work process and avoid wasting time and money on things that are not relevant to the success of the project.

The research phase of the bid

Winning the Games was a long process. It began in 1997 when the British Olympic Committee decided they wanted to bring the Olympic Games to London.

The strength of the UK Bid Team came from past disappointments: they were defeated in 1992 when they bid to host the Olympic Games in Birmingham and again when they bid for Manchester in 1996. When the IOC turned down a second bid to host the Games in Manchester in 2000, it convinced the UK team that only London, the capital, could really win if they were going to apply again.

The British Olympic Association (BOA) began to investigate sites in London where Olympic events could be held. David Luckes MBE, a former field-hockey goalkeeper who took part in the Summer Olympics for Great Britain in 1992, 1996 and 2000, was in charge of the Sport Competition for the London Organising Committee of the Olympic and Paralympic Games (the London Organising Committee). In 1997, he published a report that identified possible sites in west and east London. The BOA then began lobbying for the bid with local government, Parliament and the media to get them behind the idea that London could host the Olympics in 2012.

The original UK Bid Team

Before Lord Coe became involved as chairman, the UK bid was led by London-based American businesswoman Barbara Cassani. In 1997, Cassani founded the budget airline Go Fly under British Airways, and in 2003 she became a non-executive director of Marks & Spencer.

That same year, 1997, Cassani was appointed to chair London's bid to host the 2012 Olympic Games. Although she was unknown in the world of sport and an American, the BOA felt that Cassani would bring a professionalism to the bid that was badly needed. This followed the debacle of the UK being forced to pull out of hosting the 2005 World Athletics Championships when Britain wanted to stage the championships in Sheffield at the Don Valley Stadium instead of hosting it in London as originally proposed. Adrian Metcalfe, who was the chair of the UK Sports Major Event Group and was instrumental in London winning the right to stage the 2005 championships, said:

This decision will seriously dent any hopes of bringing the
Olympics to London in the short to medium term. The progress
we have made as a nation becomes meaningless if our
guarantees of the staging of events can be called into question.

The bidding process took place in two stages and it was Barbara Cassani who led the team through the first stage of the process. During her time as chair, she was successful in getting buy-in from politicians and a sceptical British public. Her team, focusing on the common goal of winning the 2012 Olympics for London, wrote the plan detailing where the events would be held, the infrastructure that would be required and the projected budget for the Games.

The bid was officially launched in January 2004 at the Royal Opera House in Covent Garden with presentations from the then Prime Minister Tony Blair, and the newly elected Mayor of London, Ken Livingstone. This was submitted to the IOC and, because of the work Cassani and her team had done, London moved on to the second stage of the process as one of five other possible cities to host the Games. The other cities in the running were Paris, Moscow, Madrid and New York.

In May 2004, Cassani stepped down, allowing Lord Coe to become chair for the second phase of the bidding process. Cassani said that she believed Lord Coe's record in the Olympic movement would be more useful at this point in the UK bid. She continued to serve under Lord Coe as vice-chair and advised on technical aspects of the bid.

Lord Coe, as a British athlete, world-record holder and Olympic champion, was seen as an inspirational leader. He had lived the dream and he understood the value of the Olympics. With the right skill set and experience, Lord Coe was to take the bid team through the next stage of the process.

Gaining support for the UK bid

Now that London was considered a viable contender for the 2012 Olympics, the UK Bid Team needed to get the support of the Mayor of London, Ken Livingstone. He recognised that the London bid would help regenerate the East End, which was a deprived area of the city.

The momentum grew across the country and eventually the press began to get behind the project. The first paper that really took it up was the *Daily Telegraph*. The Sports Editor at the time, the late David Welch, was a keen supporter of bringing the Olympics to London. He had seen first-hand the effect that the Games had had in Sydney in 2000, when they had captured the public's imagination.

Tessa Jowell, Secretary of State for Culture, Media and Sport at that time, took on the task of convincing the Cabinet and politicians that the London bid was a viable proposition. She was the driving force behind getting their support and emphasised that this would be much more than just seventeen days of sport: it would create a powerful legacy for generations to come.

It was crucial to bring this vision into the bid itself so that Tessa Jowell could get the backing of her colleagues for the proposal. Slowly but surely, she managed to convince her Cabinet colleagues and eventually Prime Minister Tony Blair of the benefits of hosting the Olympic Games. To convince the government ministers of the benefits, Jowell first had to convince the heads of all the different government departments that this was a win not just for her and her department but for everyone and the country as a whole.

The Bid Team wanted to create a truly transformational project for east London that would regenerate the area and leave a legacy for the people who live there. They also wanted to ensure that even though this was to be a London-based Olympics, the events would be spread nationally. By doing so, they would get the support of the rest of the country and avoid a north-south divide.

The legacy

The UK Bid Team had a shared vision. They wanted the 2012 Olympic Games to leave a legacy that would continue after the event. Their vision was to host an Olympic Games that would inspire young people – not just in London, but all over the world – to get involved in sport.

At the heart of the vision were the concepts of affordability and sustainability, and these became prime targets for the team in the bid. Sustainability is one of the three pillars of the Olympic agenda, alongside credibility and youth.

The IOC Sustainability and Legacy Commission advises the IOC Executive Board and the IOC President on sustainability and legacy matters to 'enable them to make informed, balanced decisions that maximise positive impacts, minimise negative impacts and foster positive change and legacies in the social, economic and environmental spheres.' In line with its recommendations, the IOC developed a sustainability strategy.

Given that billions of pounds would be spent on hosting seventeen days of events, the UK Bid Team wanted to be sure that the buildings and sites used would not become a burden, as had happened in other Olympic cities. For example, several venues for the 2004 Olympics in Athens in Greece fell into disrepair because Greece was unable to invest in their upkeep after it was hit hard by the global financial crisis. Similarly, many of the Olympic venues in Rio, Brazil started to fall into disrepair less than a year after staging the 2016 Olympic Games. The UK Bid Team's clear goal to leave a lasting legacy for young people and inspire them to take part in sports impressed the IOC.

The Bid Team recognised the lessons learned from the Barcelona 1992 and Sydney 2000 Olympics in regard to sustainability and legacy. They made it the main focus to create a lasting impression for future generations. Sustainability played a major role in the design of the venues in the Olympic Park. For example, the team kept the weight of the stadium structure as low as possible by reducing the amount of concrete and steel that was used. This led to a decrease in grey energy. (Grey energy is the hidden energy associated with a product, meaning the total energy consumed throughout the product's life, from its production to its disposal.) Large amounts of scrap metal were used for the stadium roof, including 2,500 tonnes of steel tubing made from old gas pipelines and even guns confiscated by the Metropolitan Police. As a result, the London 2012 stadium used only one-quarter of the weight of steel that was used to build Beijing's 'Bird's Nest' stadium.

London 2012's sustainability policy included five overarching themes to focus the Games agenda. These were climate change, waste, biodiversity, inclusion and healthy living. The mission of the Olympic Delivery Authority (ODA) was to deliver the infrastructure and venues on time and on budget while making the most of the opportunities to create a sustainable legacy for the Games. All this was incorporated into the ODA's sustainable development strategy.

Awarding the Games to London

When the IOC Evaluation Committee had visited in 2005 they had expressed how impressed they were with the UK proposal, so the UK Bid Team were in good spirits when arriving in Singapore for the final vote. Lord Coe and the rest of the hundred-strong British delegation felt that they had a good chance of winning the bid to host the Games. With the help of David Beckham and Prince William, the team worked hard to build relationships with the IOC members attending the final vote and convince them that London could host the 2012 Games.

It was then that Tessa Jowell, Ken Livingstone and Lord Coe gave one of the finest presentations ever seen by the IOC. This was the time when it mattered most. It was their moment to sway any delegate who needed further convincing that London could host the Games. Lord Coe finished by saying:

> *Today, in Britain's fourth bid in recent years, we offer London's vision of inspiration and legacy. Choose London today and you send a clear message to the youth of the world: more than ever, the Olympic Games are for you.*

When the results came out London had won, beating Paris by four votes. London was the first city ever to host the Games three times, having hosted them in 1908 and then in 1948. The UK had put sustainability and legacy at the heart of its bid, and that was what helped it win.

The winning announcement was made on 6 July 2005. On 7 July London was bombed by terrorists and fifty-two people lost their lives. This tragedy might have made the team even more determined to put on the best Games possible for the people of London and the UK.

The UK Bid Team had presented a fresh vision to the IOC for the Olympic Games. They planned to use interesting venues, with London taking centre stage. They showed the old British bulldog spirit of determination and passion for one common goal, and this was what the Olympic Committee picked up on. In March 2006, the London Olympic Games and the Paralympic Games received royal assent and the Olympic Delivery Authority (ODA), a publicly accountable body, was created. The ODA had the power to buy land and agree the building required for London 2012.

Now, time was of the essence.

The London Olympics were to be held on industrial wasteland, so there was much preparatory work to do to get it ready before the building work could start. Services, such as water and electricity, had to be diverted and businesses bought up and relocated. Given that the Olympic stadium was to be built in the East End of London, the transport systems had to be improved to make sure people could get to the venues. This was all part of ensuring that the London Games would be a success and meet the needs of local communities long after the event ended.

Team Stadium

The timescale was very short from winning the bid to the Games taking place in London. The Olympic stadium, the aquatics centre and the velodrome, among other venues and facilities, had to be built.

The UK bid organisers needed to choose a delivery team with proven ability and a good record, who could design and build venues on budget and within the set timescales. They looked at the team that had successfully completed the Arsenal Emirates Stadium in London in 2006 at a cost of £390 million. That team had consisted of the architects Populous, the structural engineers BuroHappold and the main contractor Sir Robert McAlpine. Populous had also worked on the Sydney Olympics Telstra Stadium, so they brought valuable experience from that project to London. Given the provenance and experience of this team, the ODA chose it to manage the project of building the stadium for London 2012.

Because the ODA was a publicly accountable body, certain checks and balances had to be included in the design and construction process to ensure that the stadium met the legacy requirements and objectives set for the London Olympic Games. These included sustainability goals and the need to make sure that the venues were not built merely for profit.

A series of teams and advisors audited the objectives set for the Games. One of these was the third-party checker. The third-party checker's task was to confirm that the concept and design of the Olympic stadium and the other venues were safe, affordable and kept to the brief and requirements set by the ODA and the IOC.

At that time, I worked for NRM Bobrowski, a structural engineering consultancy that was bought by Capita Symonds in 2008. NRM Bobrowski won the bid to be the third-party checkers for the Olympic stadium and the aquatic centre. This company had many years of experience in designing and delivering sports and leisure projects. These included football stands, such as the North Stand at Ipswich Town Football Club, and stands at Cheltenham, Sandown and Newmarket racecourses.

Within the work that NRM Bobrowski was doing, my role was to lead the team of third-party checkers carrying out the detailed design checks on BuroHappold's work for the London 2012 Olympic stadium. The detailed third-party design checks, which I managed for the Olympic stadium, lasted approximately four years throughout the design and construction phases of the stadium.

This newly formed London 2012 project team, Team Stadium, took the goal of creating a lasting legacy for future generations from dream to reality.

Lessons learned

Each member of the UK Bid Team, no matter what their role or when they joined the project, signed up to the vision of achieving a lasting legacy, not only for London but also for young people around the UK and the world. Their aim was to inspire young people to take part in sport and to leave an enduring legacy of infrastructure, buildings and, more importantly, an ideal.

In any building project, big or small, it is key to have a common goal that the whole team agree to work towards and believe in. Accepting this principle will ensure the success of the project, just as it ensured the success of the UK in its bid for the 2012 Olympic Games.

Every member of a team has their strong points, but weaving those strengths into a team that has a common goal and ambition in its understanding of what the project stands for is what brings about success.

CHAPTER 2
THE IMPORTANCE OF PLANNING

If you fail to plan, you are planning to fail.

Benjamin Franklin

The importance of planning

The importance of planning a building project can never be overstated, and this is the basis of my second principle of running a successful project. Proper planning is central to the success of any project of any scale. Without a plan, you are almost doomed to failure.

Some things may go right when there is no proper planning, but this is more by chance than down to judgement or properly focused effort. In business, it is prudent to do things cost-effectively. The output of the business needs to be delivered on

View of the London 2012 Olympic Stadium
on the island site with connecting bridges.

time and on budget. Without a good plan, this is unlikely to happen, as the team has a poor understanding of the resources needed, how to keep to the timescale and what objectives are to be achieved. As a consequence, time and energy are wasted and resources are unlikely to be used efficiently or effectively. Poor delivery and a substandard service always risk ruining a company's reputation with a client.

PRINCIPLE 2: DEVELOP A GOOD, DETAILED PLAN BEFORE YOU START

A good detailed plan will help you do the following:
- Give direction and focus to a project.
- Make the timescales clear for the important goals and milestones.
- List the resources needed to achieve the objectives.
- Assess the skills needed to achieve the objectives.
- Make clear how to deliver the project.
- Build a solid reputation for providing a high-quality, cost-effective service.

In the next section, I discuss the importance of planning in relation to the success of the Olympic stadium. I explain how the team was chosen to meet the tight timescales and demands of the project and how the architect and engineer worked together to design and build a structure that would meet the needs of the Olympics and those who would continue to use it after the event.

The architectural scheme

The organisers of the London 2012 Olympic Games were certainly not looking to make life easy for the architect of the Olympic stadium when they chose Stratford, an area of east London in desperate need of regeneration, as the site. With the goal of creating a legacy for generations to come, 300 hectares of century-old industrial contaminated land would have to be cleared, along with 2 million tonnes of contaminated soil, before the building could begin. On top of that, the organisers had to design a stadium that could be reduced from 80,000 seats to 25,000 seats after the Games. Although the architect, Populous, had worked on the Sydney Olympic stadium (which was reduced from 115,000 seats to 83,000 seats), the scale of conversion proposed for London had never been attempted before.

Because the site for the stadium was surrounded by rivers, canals and railway lines, it was known as an island site. The physical constraints of the island site added to the challenge, as the first studies of comparable stadiums indicated that they would not fit on the site.

The starting point for Populous was to consider the whole island as a stadium, with spectators effectively entering as they walked over one of five new bridges proposed to connect the island with the rest of the Olympic Park. They then considered how they could use the topography of the site (its natural and manmade physical features) to accommodate the split of temporary and permanent seating.

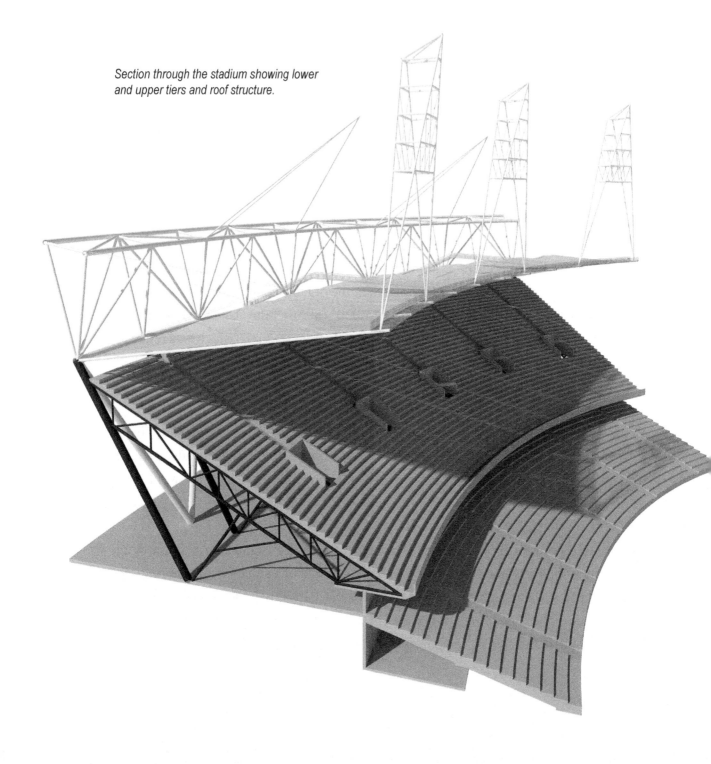

Section through the stadium showing lower and upper tiers and roof structure.

The 6-metre fall across the site from north to south allowed for a 'cut and fill' approach, which meant forming a permanent landscaped bowl in the earth for the 25,000 permanent seats and building a separate temporary structure above for the 55,000 temporary seats. This had the added benefit of separating athletes and the media (who would be located on the lower ground at the level of the track) from spectators, who could enjoy level access across the bridges straight into the stadium.

Another benefit of having some of the seating sunken in this way was to bring the spectators closer to the action. This would create the atmosphere of excitement that helped the athletes perform at their best during the Games.

The main features of the Olympic stadium were as follows:

The stadium bowl: a bowl sunken into the ground for the field of play and lower permanent seating, designed to bring spectators close to the action.

Seating: 25,000 permanent seats and 55,000 demountable seats, giving a total of 80,000 seats.

Roof: a cable-supported roof that would stretch 28 metres around the stadium, providing cover for two-thirds of the spectators.

Wrap: a fabric curtain hung in sections that would wrap around the stadium structure, giving more protection and shelter for spectators.

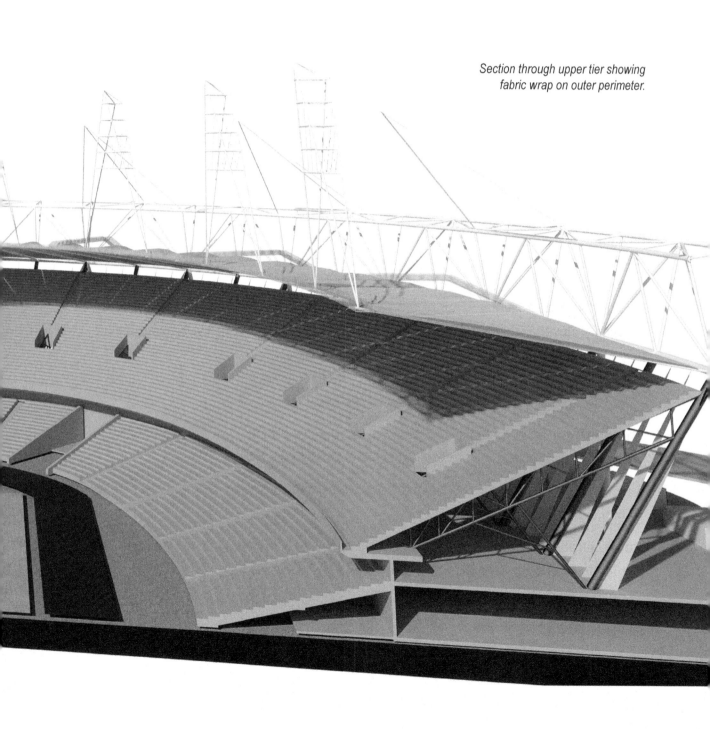

Section through upper tier showing
fabric wrap on outer perimeter.

Pods: facilities, such as food outlets and shops, were grouped in self-contained pod structures, adding to the spectator experience around the access level of the stadium.

As mentioned before, the architectural team were chosen mainly because they had worked on previous stadiums, in particular the Olympic stadium in Sydney. That stadium was similar to the proposed stadium in London in that it had a temporary element to it. After the Games, the Sydney stadium was reduced from 115,000 seats to 83,000 seats.

In London, the Olympic stadium would have 80,000 seats. It would be the centrepiece of the Olympic Games, where the opening and closing ceremonies and the athletic events would be held. Once the Games were finished, the stadium was to be reduced to 25,000 seats and become a new home for athletics and other sports, community and educational uses. An Olympic stadium with such a large demountable element had never been attempted before. It represented the start of a new era for Olympic stadium design, with a combination of temporary and permanent elements providing the high-level performance needed for a major sports event while meeting the long-term needs of the community.

Given this need for temporary structures wedded with permanent structures, the Olympic bid organisers wanted an experienced architectural team that could work with this specification within the tight timescales ahead.

Senior Principal Architect at Populous Rob Sheard had personal experience of working on the Sydney Olympic stadium. He had also worked on the Yankee Stadium in New York. He said that the design of the London Olympic stadium was 'a response to the challenge of creating the temporary and permanent at the same time' that showed 'how a successful event can be blended with the long-term needs of the community'.

The team as a whole – the architect, engineer and contractor – had all worked together on the Emirates Stadium in London. As such, they not only had the right experience but also were used to working with each other. This blend of shared experience was fundamental to achieving the planned programme of work, as time was short.

It was also necessary to consider how to provide the spectator facilities (such as toilets and food outlets) in a temporary building. To respond to the strong sustainability agenda and minimise the costs of transforming the stadium after the Games, the architects decided to move most of the spectator facilities outside the stadium and locate them in self-contained pods around the island. These pods (which were eventually replaced by conventional temporary catering units of a lightweight construction) were grouped in villages, which allowed spectators to enjoy the ambiance of the park setting as well as the athletics. By pulling these facilities out of the main body of the stadium, the architects dramatically reduced the scale and mass of the building and created a far more intimate seating bowl, with spectators much closer to the track than in similar stadiums.

The International Association of Athletics Federations (IAAF) set strict requirements for the track and field. Populous worked within these guidelines to plan a compact layout that added to the intimacy of the seating bowl.

The fabric wrap

Having established a general form and mass for the stadium, the architect explored the question of the building envelope.

The architect considered traditional forms of construction to be inappropriate and unnecessary for a temporary structure. To find a more appropriate way of providing the building envelope, the team took inspiration from the stage sets used in outdoor events and designed the stadium to be cloaked in a lightweight fabric wrap. The sections of fabric wrap were designed to run from the roof and twist at the base. This would allow spectators to enter the seating bowl at any point around its perimeter.

The architects worked with artist Sophie Smallhorn, who integrated the colours of the London 2012 brand into the design of the circulation route. This helped to make the stadium an international symbol for London and the 2012 Olympic Games.

The roof

The architect created several designs for the roof to explore flexibility in transforming the stadium and providing appropriate conditions for athletic events. One of the

IAAF's criteria was to shield the track from the effects of wind: if the wind speed is greater than 2 metres a second at track level, any records set on the track and assisted by the wind are not upheld.

This meant it was crucial for the design team to minimise wind speed at track level. To find the best solution to this problem, the team carried out parametric studies of several options for the roof layout. Early ideas for hinge sections of the roof, which adjusted the extent of roof cover over the seating, proved too expensive, while a standard cantilever solution struggled to cater for the servicing (sports lighting and ceremonies) requirements of the Games. Ultimately a fabric roof, based on the engineering principles of a bicycle wheel, proved to be the best overall solution. It provided an appropriate area of lightweight roof cover, while accommodating the requirements for sports lighting and ceremonies.

The architect also worked closely with the London Organising Committee to integrate the brand identity into the colour of the track and the pattern of the seats. This ensured that the stadium provided an instantly recognisable backdrop for the London 2012 Games.

The opening ceremony

The delivery team started designing the Olympic stadium for London 2012 five years before the opening ceremony. A director had not yet been appointed, so the design team were working in the dark. They needed to make assumptions about what might be required for the opening ceremony and include them in the original design. To do this, it is likely that they researched what had been included in the design of other Olympic stadiums and in other opening and closing ceremonies.

Most opening ceremonies have plenty of moving features. They are not just a visual display; they create movement and atmosphere. The design team needed to consider these important aspects in the early planning stages, making assumptions about what moving features might be included in such a ceremony and taking account of their weight and flow. During the planning phase, they had to include structural elements that would make the creative ideas for the opening ceremony a reality, even though those ideas were, as yet, unknown.

Forming an effective team

Having the right team at the right place at the right time made a big contribution to the success of the Olympic stadium. With any new team, time needs to be spent at the beginning getting to know each other, identifying each other's strengths and weaknesses and working out the best ways to work together. This is a normal part of team development. As the design team had worked together before on the Emirates Stadium, this learning curve, for the most part, was bypassed. Once the bid was won, the design team started work immediately, knowing it had four years to come up with a design so the building could start.

For any building project of this size, the architect designs the layout. They set out the stadium, its size and its proportions. It is then up to the engineer to interpret the design to create a functional structural scheme. In the case of the Olympic stadium, because the architect and engineer had worked together before, the architect could save time by anticipating the consequences of some of the design decisions that the engineer would make.

It is the structural engineer's job to make everything stand up and work physically, but they have to take account of how the architect wants the building to look. This successful merging and fusion of form between the architect and the engineer was clearly shown in the quality of the finished Olympic stadium. Many people have complimented the way it blended the structural and architectural elements: it was functional yet aesthetically pleasing, and both elements contributed to its overall look and form.

When the design of the Olympic stadium was unveiled, ODA Chair John Armitt said:

> *London's Olympic Stadium is designed to be different. Team Stadium have done a fantastic job against a challenging brief. The innovative, ground-breaking design will ensure that the Olympic Stadium will not only be a fantastic arena for a summer of sport in 2012 but also ensure a sustainable legacy for the community who will live around it.*

Chair of the London Organising Committee Sebastian Coe said:

> *We talk a lot about milestones, but few will be more exciting than this unveiling of the Olympic Stadium, which will be the centrepiece of our Olympic Park. The Stadium will stand for everything we talked about in the bid: it will be inspiring, innovative and sustainable – the theatre within which the Olympic Games and Paralympic Games will be played out and leaving behind top class sporting and community facilities after the Games. We genuinely believe that this creates a new blueprint for building Olympic stadiums – one which integrates the Games time requirements with a long-term legacy vision.*

Knowing that the legacy element of the design was an essential requirement meant that the architect and engineer had to build this into the design from day one.

Upfront planning prevents future problems

A stadium the size of the one in London was likely to become unwanted after the event. This had happened in other cities that had hosted the Olympic Games. The need to learn from these past events shows the importance of good research. This ensured that the objectives set for the Olympic stadium were correct from the outset.

By setting the fundamental criteria and goals at the beginning of the project, Team Stadium was able to build these into the design from the start.

Right from the beginning, the architect and engineer worked together to get the small details right. Thorough planning enabled them to pre-empt many problems and find solutions early. For example, knowing that a wind speed stronger than 2 metres per second could render an athlete's result invalid led to choosing the right option for the roof in the early planning phase. They considered the comfort of spectators during the planning phase too, deciding that the roof would stretch across 28 metres to cover two-thirds of the spectators and that the fabric wrap would provide extra protection.

From the start, Team Stadium planned for the post-Olympic conversion from 80,000 seats to 25,000 seats. There were two parts to this plan. The first was the oval concrete bowl, which was sunken into the ground and provided permanent seating. This was an independent structure, which would be left behind as part of the legacy. The second part included the independent structures for the upper tiers and the roof. Right from the beginning, these were planned as temporary structures because the team knew they would be taken down.

The clearly visible V-shaped steel supports acted as bracing, giving stability to the upper parts of the stadium and helping to support the steel truss roof structure (called the compression ring) for the roof. This supported the delicate cable construction that held the lightweight fabric roof at the top.

A special feature was the simple way of removing the second structure, which was designed during the planning phase. The team designed all the connections to be bolted rather than welded, similar to a Meccano set, so it could be taken apart easily.

Lessons learned

To write a successful plan, you should consider these key things:

1 **Get a detailed brief before you start and make sure you fully understand the client's requirements.** Once you know what the client's requirements are, you can use them to set all the important goals and milestones of the plan. These will include not only the physical aspects of the structure or building but also the timescales, the budget and other key criteria. These requirements become the roadmap of the plan and influence the outcomes and duration of each part of the project to be delivered.

2 **Monitor the plan as you go.** Plans need to be monitored and updated to reflect how the real progress and order of production compare with those predicted at the outset. You might need to make minor adjustments, especially to how you allocate resources, to maintain the desired rate of progress. If a plan is not monitored and compared with the actual rate of progress and production, it is worthless. That said, even with the best laid plans the unexpected can happen and derail the smooth running of a project. Because of this, you need to make your plan flexible enough to accommodate and deal with unexpected events. You will

need to be able to speedily develop a plan B to assess how the unexpected event affects your original plan.

3   **Know when to ask for help.** No one is an expert in everything, regardless of their profession or qualifications. They may be the best in their field of expertise, but it is vital to the success of the project to have the right expertise available. For example, while designing the Olympic stadium, for the fabric roof design the structural engineers used experts that they had within the company. They were specialists in that field and contributed to the success of that part of the building.

4   **Don't reinvent the wheel.** Where possible, research successful examples of the type of project you are working on. Look for examples of best practice. If it has been done before, you might be able to learn lessons from the experiences of those involved and apply them to your current project.

No matter how successful we are in our field of business, we should all be constantly learning new things. If we are unable or unwilling to learn then our development will be stalled. Having said this, no one can know everything, so a team needs the input of many people to overcome this deficiency.

5   **Use all the available resources.** Resources are available within a company and outside it. Externally and internally, your peers are a source of good-quality information and advice. You might also be able to find some common ground for help from a competitor.

Attention to detail in the planning stage makes the difference to the success of a project, so this must be planned for right from the beginning. Team Stadium proved that, with detailed planning and early identification of any issues, they were able to meet the legacy objectives of the Olympic bid and build a stadium that Lord Coe said in 2012 would be remembered as 'inspiring, innovative and sustainable'.

Applying the key factors that contribute to successful planning as soon as you begin a project will allow you to complete your product or design within the timescales, within budget and to high standard.

London 2012 would not have been as successful if everyone involved had not worked together to develop a good, detailed plan right from the start of the project. It was important to get a clear understanding of the legacy that was to be left after the Games and to work together effectively to identify problems early and decide on the best solutions.

Key to this success was getting the right people in the right positions in the right team, planning together from the start.

CHAPTER 3
COMMUNICATION:
THE KEY TO SUCCESS

*The biggest problem in communication is the illusion that
it has taken place.*

George Bernard Shaw

The importance of good communication

Have you worked on a project where you thought you understood the brief but found
halfway through that you were on the wrong track? Maybe you can remember projects
that have gone over time and budget because of bad communication between architects,
engineers and the client. Good communication is essential to any successful project,
and it is our third principle of running a successful project.

PRINCIPLE 3: DEVELOP A GOOD COMMUNICATION STRATEGY

If you have a good communication strategy in place right from the start of the project, your team members will:

- understand their roles clearly
- know what their responsibilities are
- understand what others expect from them, and
- know the timescale they need to work within.

With an effective communication strategy in place, information will flow naturally. Without this, delays can happen and put the whole project behind. If open communication is achieved among the team, the project will progress at a much faster pace with fewer risks involved.

When the Olympic stadium was completed, Sir John Armitt, Chair of the ODA said, 'We have proved that Britain can deliver a construction and civil engineering project of this size, on time and on budget.' At the heart of its success was a communication strategy that took account of essentials:

- Having the right team in place
- Knowing timescales and budget
- Being clear on key deliverables.

In this chapter, I discuss what makes a good communication strategy, how the communication strategy contributed to the success of the design, and how you might implement this in your own practice.

What makes a good communication strategy?

You know when a team has achieved an effective communication structure when everyone involved in the project:

- knows what they are doing
- knows where they are at any point during the project, and
- can get the information they need in a timely way from decision makers.

A strategy that encourages open but questioning communication and creates a no-blame culture prevents hidden agendas developing between those involved. It also reduces the number of risks that are left unidentified and problems left undiscovered. Open communication helps make sure that risks and delays are identified as soon as they occur and plans are put in place quickly to resolve these issues.

As in any industry, construction clients don't like surprises, as they usually end up costing time and money. On projects of such a scale as the London 2012 Olympic stadium, regular design team meetings (where the whole team get together) are a key part of the communication strategy. These meetings allow you to find out what stage team members are at and compare this with where you expected them to be at that point in the programme. The meetings can be solution-focused, identifying ways to do things more efficiently, or they can look at whether you need to bring in particular specialists or skills to resolve a specific issue.

All members of Team Stadium knew that the goal of the London 2012 Olympic bid was to regenerate the East End by including the ideals of sustainability and legacy and inspiring younger generations to take part in sport. London proposed a new type of experience for the Games – the organisers acknowledged the interest in and the spirit of the event itself, but they also wanted to leave a legacy.

What would happen after the Games was a high priority and an important consideration right from the beginning of the design process. The communication strategy at the heart of the London Olympic project brought out the best of the team involved, enabling them to come up with a design that was structurally feasible. As Senior Principal Architect at Populous Rob Sheard said:

> *The design is a response to the challenge of creating the temporary and the permanent at the same time – that is the essence of the design for the Stadium. A new era of Olympic Stadium design will be launched in 2012, demonstrating how a successful event can be blended with the long-term needs of the community.*

The structural scheme

In April 2008 Team Stadium were appointed as an integrated design and construction team for the main stadium. From the beginning, Team Stadium worked closely with the client through the ODA to develop and interpret the brief.

This close communication about converting the strategic goals of the bid into a reality resulted in all members of the team believing that they were delivering a stadium that was fit for the London 2012 Olympic and Paralympic Games. It was a key aspect of the success of the whole project.

The use of an integrated design and construction team was similar to a project that I worked on in 2001 – the design and construction of the new 7,500-seat North Stand at Ipswich Town Football Club. This was also dominated by a tight schedule, because the work on site did not start until the end of the 2000–2001 football season but the stand had to be ready for the next season.

It was clear to the design team that to achieve this goal, they needed to consider the following aspects:

- Having sections of the stand prefabricated to make it easier to assemble.
- Minimising the use of applied finishes.
- Using material that is inherently fire resistant.
- Making the erection of the stand easier and quicker by minimising the number of components that made up the stand.

Ipswich Town Football Club North Stand - one of Derek's projects.

These considerations meant that precast concrete was chosen for the project. This was reflected in the structural design, which is essentially precast concrete strengthened by in-situ stitches, toppings, steel beams and a steel roof.

It became clear early in the design process that manufacturing quality and tolerance control (to ensure everything fitted) were going to be critical to completing the required programme. The number and complexity of interfaces between the precast concrete and steelwork, combined with the need for continuous co-ordination between the suppliers and erection crew, led to the conclusion that there should be one subcontracted package for the supply and build of the entire structure.

As a result, a lead frame contractor was appointed for the whole package. This was negotiated from the start on an open-book basis. (An open-book policy is an agreement to view data and financial information about costs incurred in any one part of the supply chain for the contract.) This allowed the earliest possible specialist input into the design process and gave continuity to the construction site.

The benefits of using this approach were similar to those of using the integrated design and construction team approach for the Olympic stadium. Having this integrated team from the beginning of the project meant that all members of Team Stadium could work together to refine the design and process early on. This meant that they did not have to spend time redesigning at a later date and cause unnecessary delays.

Because the stadium was a prominent Olympic venue, a state-of-the-art facility was needed for the media, spectators and athletes. It had to be a flexible, multi-faceted venue capable of accommodating world-class athletics, national (UK) athletes and elite athletes with disabilities. It had to be able to accommodate other events, such as football and rugby, contests, and community sports and cultural events.

This was a real challenge for the design. Stadiums had been converted before, but nothing on the scale proposed for the London 2012 stadium had been attempted. The construction needed to be reusable, relocatable and recyclable wherever possible to meet the legacy and the sustainability goals of the Olympic bid. The post-Games stadium was to be appropriate for permanent sports, it had to be durable, and it had to involve low maintenance and energy costs.

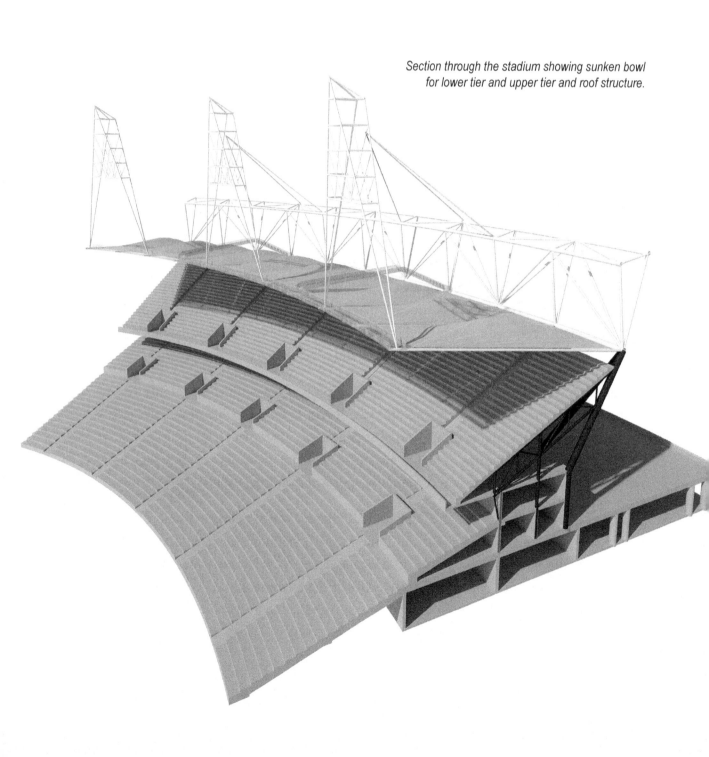

Section through the stadium showing sunken bowl for lower tier and upper tier and roof structure.

Assessing the East End site, the seating bowl, the stadium size and the roof were crucial in developing the overall form of the stadium. The site chosen was an unusual one, as it was an island site. Good communication between all the team members was essential to ensure that the architectural and engineering requirements for the stadium were achieved within the island site. This was done by having the regular team meetings and communicating effectively throughout the design phase.

The seating bowl

The seating bowl was a single, uniform tier that was sunken into the landscape to form the seating section for the Games. It was made for the 25,000 permanent seats and was constructed of precast concrete.

The temporary structure for the 55,000 seats was the upper tier. It was clear that this solution would make the conversion simple and clear. The team chose concrete, a conventional material, for the lower bowl, which gave it a durable, permanent feel. At first the team envisaged that the upper tier would be constructed from scaffold, but that was later changed to a steel structure.

'Embracing the temporary' was the single most important decision in the design development. This extended to placing most of the spectator facilities outside the stadium in self-contained pods around the island. Doing this dramatically reduced the scale and mass of the building, as well as the embodied energy (the energy used by all the processes involved in building the stadium, from extracting the raw materials to transporting them and using them in construction) of the construction.

This design met the strong sustainability agenda set by London 2012 and helped to minimise the costs of transforming the stadium after the Games. It also enabled the stadium to fit on the island site with enough areas around it for people to move about, whereas a stadium of a conventional size would have been unable to fit on the site.

The bowl steelwork was engineered for the temporary tiers. The early engineering concepts involved using scaffold-type supports for the upper tier, but it became clear that scaffold tubing, while being a more temporary way of doing things, would not have suited the look of the stadium in the way the architect wanted, so the team decided on a conventional steel structure.

The perimeter section of columns in the stadium were steeply inclined. These were the distinctive white sloping columns that created the recognisable look of the stadium. They also had a functional purpose, because the sloping columns formed the bracing for the compression ring around the top of the stadium for the roof. This design also created more entry points to the stadium for spectators; there were fifty-six entry points in total. Because it was an island site, there were some areas where Team Stadium needed to build up the embankments by using reinforced earth to make it easier for people to move around it.

While developing the concepts for the design, Team Stadium recognised that the stadium's location on an island site would allow the security lines to be on the bridges, away from the stadium. This helped to control the crowd and improve security, which was a crucial factor in the whole design. It also allowed for the perfect light design of the stadium perimeter, and the architects were able to explore using a wrap for the external façade (the temporary fabric wrap described in Chapter 2). The steelwork for the upper tier was painted black, while the sloping supporting columns were white. This contrast helped to create a journey through a black space towards views of the track and the field areas.

Wind-engineering studies

The team needed to carry out wind-engineering studies so they could carefully consider whether a roof was needed for such a temporary event. The engineers did these studies early in the design stage so they could define the size of the roof from the beginning. To do this, they developed a 3D virtual wind tunnel to measure wind performance against a number of factors, including the roof area. This allowed the team to make a quick decision on a range of options at the primary design stage. Later on, they made a real model of the stadium for wind-tunnel tests to get more data and test the accuracy of the virtual studies.

The studies considered winds with a speed of more than 2 metres per second and the general comfort of athletes and spectators. The engineers carried out most of the wind-direction studies without a roof covering, with the wind rising up over

View from inside the completed stadium showing the seating tiers, roof and structure above.

the stadium and recirculating air within the stadium. Then they introduced a partial roof covering to reduce the roof opening, with a small area over which to drive this recirculation. This reduced the wind speed in the stadium. The study results showed that a partial covering of a specific size gave enough protection and reduced wind speeds at track level.

The engineers presented the results of the studies to the client shortly after a very windy pre-athletics meeting, where the athletes had commented on the blustery nature of the event. The client did not want complaints from Olympic athletes about similar conditions in the Olympic stadium; neither did they want the wind to have a negative effect on records set in the stadium. Because of the complaints at the affected athletics meeting, the client was open to the wind specialists' proposals and together they chose a partial roof. The purpose of the roof was not to shield spectators from the rain; it was only to minimise the effect of wind on the track. Although some shelter from rain was possible, the size of the roof covering was dictated solely by wind engineering.

The detailed costing and programming for the roof engineering was carried out for two alternative designs: a cable-net roof and a steel cantilever roof. The engineers looked at a range of factors to measure the effectiveness of each design in parallel with the wind-engineering study. They also reviewed two designs to support the roof to see where they could save time on the programme. The results of all of these studies led to the cable-net option being chosen, which partly covered the stand.

The team worked intensively with the ODA to develop early strategies for adding a rigging system to the cable net for the opening and closing ceremonies. The team believed that this was one of the few times in the history of the modern Olympic Games when this co-ordination took place at such an early stage. As mentioned earlier, Team Stadium had to make certain assumptions about the ceremonies. They studied past Olympic Games and their opening and closing ceremonies to estimate the kinds of loads that might be expected and incorporate these at the early design stage.

The final result was an innovative lightweight stadium that could be reduced from 80,000 seats to 25,000 seats after the Games so it could be used for local athletics events. The design response met a challenging brief in an unusual, distinct and elegant way.

Although the approach of running two or three different designs in parallel is not unusual in a project of this size, because of the importance of the Olympic stadium – and the need to complete it within budget and on time – this was an ideal approach. Team Stadium had to come up with the best solution that they could within the timeframe allowed. To do this, part of the team worked on one portion of the roof to design one scheme and another part of the team designed the other scheme. They worked together to a degree, and communicated their findings and design solutions to each other, but they had two separate teams for two distinct designs. Then, with the wind-engineering studies, they were able to do an accurate cost analysis.

Good communication was the essence in making this approach work; in particular, communicating with the contracting side to get accurate costings. Obviously, being able to construct the stadium quickly, efficiently and cost-effectively all came into to the decision about which was the best solution.

Lessons learned

1   Consider the team location. One of the main reasons the Olympic stadium was finished ahead of time and within budget was the success of the communication strategy, which was in place from the beginning of the decision to appoint the members of Team Stadium. At the core of this strategy was the fact that all the team worked together in the same building – not only the architects, engineers, contractors and mechanical engineers but also the client's representatives. Given that the client is usually in a separate building and only speaks to the architects, this was unusual. It meant that the client was involved in all discussions, not just with the architects but also with the structural engineers and the mechanical engineers.

Although there were monthly design meetings, the team didn't have to wait for these to make important decisions because communication happened every day. This led to fewer delays and faster decision making. In this scenario, Team Stadium worked with an informed client who knew what they wanted to achieve and had the authority to make decisions quickly.

2 **Use technology.** Everyone had access to documents, presentations and the latest drawings and designs, which were easily downloaded from a main server. There's nothing worse than realising that you are working on an outdated drawing because someone hasn't given you their latest drawings. The team's computer system would notify all the relevant people when new drawings were uploaded. Having up-to-date information contributed to faster decision-making.

3 **Apply previous experience.** Team Stadium had worked together on the Arsenal Stadium and brought many of the systems and procedures they had used to the Olympic stadium project. The Arsenal Stadium had been delivered on time and on budget – as a tried-and-tested team, they were chosen for the London 2012 project.

With the right communication strategy in place, any project can be as successful as the Olympic stadium project. Good communication should be at the core of every business, and keeping the client up to date is key to maintaining good relationships and a professional reputation. Even if it is bad news, it is still better for the client to know what is going on than to be kept in the dark. Lack of information breeds insecurity, and it is often the 'not knowing' that causes the client to lose confidence in a designer or contractor.

This means that communication with the client needs to be open, clear, timely and honest. An open communication culture begins with your first meeting with your client. Put everything on the table right from the start. Get the ground rules sorted so that you, your client and your team know exactly what is expected. Be clear with your client and explain to them what you are going to do, how you will do it and whether you can meet their expectations and goals. If there is something that you don't understand, that you have missed or that has not been communicated to you, bring it out up front. Your client will appreciate your open approach.

Make sure you thoroughly understand your brief from the client. Ask the client as many questions as possible to make sure that they as well as you are clear about the brief – if communication is not right, it may be because the client is thinking one thing and the architect and the engineers are thinking another. Remember that the only silly question is the one you don't ask. If you ask ten questions and nine of them appear to be silly, the tenth one could give you the missing information that changes the whole design of the project.

Make sure you understand the client's expectations of what you can do. A client may be expecting a Rolls Royce but only wants to pay the price of a Mini. There are, unfortunately, no free lunches. You get what you pay for. But it is vital for you and your client to have the same understanding and expectations about the project and what will be delivered. At the end of your conversation with the client, summarise your understanding of what they want. This gives the client the opportunity to tell you if your understanding is correct.

CHAPTER 4
GOOD TEAMWORK

Teamwork is the ability to work together towards a common vision. The ability to direct individual accomplishments toward organisational objectives. It is the fuel that allows common people to attain uncommon results.

Andrew Carnegie

The importance of good teamwork

Good teamwork is essential for a successful project. Without it, a team will not pull together, conflict will set in and competing views will slow down the plan. This all makes it less likely that the project will be completed within the time and budget set.

In 2012, Team Stadium showed how the principle of good teamwork contributed to the stadium being built on time and within budget.

PRINCIPLE 4: DEVELOP THE ETHOS OF GOOD TEAMWORK

In this chapter I explain how creating an atmosphere in which a team can flourish enables, as Andrew Carnegie says, 'common people to attain uncommon results'. We will look at what behaviours and actions create a good team ethos.

Using the development of the architectural scheme of the Olympic stadium, I look at how Team Stadium followed the principle of good teamwork throughout the life of the project.

The components of a good team

It is likely that you have experienced what it is like to work in a team that does not function well. A malfunctioning team can be devastating for a building project because, in construction, time is money.

If a project is delayed because people do not pull their weight or do not meet agreed deadlines, this will have an impact on everyone else involved. And it is that knock-on effect that ruins reputations, because you are only as good as your last project.

There are six components of a good team:

1 Every member knows, understands and believes in the common goal. They know what the end result should be and they work together to achieve it.

2 Everyone knows, recognises and understands their position in the team and what their obligations and responsibilities are.

3 Every member understands everyone else's roles and responsibilities and know what to expect from them.

4 The team members respect each other's skills and experience.

5 They are encouraged to challenge ideas and do so with respect.

6 They deal with disagreements quickly and effectively.

The architect, Populous, led the project from a design perspective, working alongside the engineers. Although the architect specified the design, the engineers also came up with ideas. Following the principles of good teamwork enabled them to share ideas, explore solutions to problems and work in unison to achieve the common goal.

The architect could not create the design successfully alone. They needed the engineers and all the other contractors involved to bring their expertise to the table and pull together. This created an atmosphere where the strengths of each member of the team were appreciated and used to their fullest. The team members challenged each other, testing ideas to identify the best ways to meet the shared goals of sustainability and creating a lasting legacy.

Testing ideas against the goal was key to Ben Hunt-Davis and his eight-man rowing team winning the gold medal in the 2000 Olympics. In Ben's book, *Will It Make the Boat go Faster?* he tells how in the four years leading up to the Olympics the team and coaches tested everything they did against the mantra of 'Will it make the boat go faster?' They realised, just as Team Stadium did, that the team was more than the sum of its individual parts.

Following the principles of good teamwork enabled them to challenge ideas effectively and develop solutions to achieve their goal. The individual members of the team did not always agree, but by communicating openly and concentrating on the core objectives, they were able to focus on what mattered.

The detailed architectural scheme

The architecture of the Olympic stadium was not flamboyant, particularly in comparison with the Beijing 2008 stadium. If you look at the two Olympic stadiums, you will see that the Beijing stadium was built on a very grand scale while the London one was not. This was a conscious decision that reflected the ideals of sustainability and leaving a legacy for future generations, which were at the heart of the London 2012 bid. The architecture was central to building a foundation for development and regeneration that would continue long after the Games had finished. Part of that vision was to be able to convert the seating capacity of the stadium from 80,000 seats to 25,000 seats so that it could be used by the local community for athletics and other events.

Credit must be given to Team Stadium for achieving this goal, as few Olympic Games in the past have managed to do this. Their excellent teamwork helped them to design and build a stadium that would never become a white elephant. This meant that London 2012 was much more about system than spectacle.

The sustainability of the architecture was key in realising this ambition as good teamwork between the different members of the team enabled this to be achieved. For example, if you compare the steel weight of the London Olympic stadium with Beijing's 'Bird's Nest' stadium, you will find that it is a quarter of the weight of the Beijing stadium. By careful and clever design, the architect and engineer for London 2012 managed to keep the weight of the steelwork down.

The sustainability and legacy goals for the London 2012 Olympic Games meant that only eight of the thirty-six London venues used for the Games were permanent new-build venues. This had never been done before in any Olympic Games.

The stadium bowl

The architect, Populous, had a difficult site to work with. It was a 40-acre site that was effectively an island. Because it was a small site surrounded by water on three sides it limited the space available for the stadium (its volume footprint). It was much smaller than the footprint of the 2000 Sydney Olympic stadium, which Populous had also worked on. Good teamwork between the architect and engineer enabled them

3D aerial image of stadium including podium.

to fit the design into the site, the architect sank the bowl of 25,000 permanent seats into the soft clay of the ground and moved the catering and retail facilities into pods outside the stadium.

The bowl formed the track and field arena. The 25,000 permanent seats were built using concrete rakers. Spectators entered the stadium at podium level, which was at the top of the permanent seating bowl. The lightweight steel and precast concrete upper tier of 55,000 seats started at the top of this permanent bowl.

The sunken oval bowl was made of concrete that contained 40% less embodied carbon (the carbon dioxide emitted during the manufacture, transport and construction of building materials, together with end of life emissions) than ordinary concrete, which helped the team meet the sustainability criteria. The team planned the stadium beautifully to create good lines of sight and provide ways to escape. They positioned the facilities for media coverage and so on below the suspended podium. This kept to the strict standards and requirements of Olympic events, including those for security.

The perimeter of the site was created at podium level. Separating the catering and retail outlets from the stadium itself reduced the fire load (to establish the potential severity of a hypothetical future fire, the heat output per unit floor area, often in kJ/m2, is calculated from the calorific value of the materials present) and ventilation requirements for the stadium structure. Having the pods outside also made it easier to stock them with food and drink – it only had to be brought to the perimeter, cutting down on congestion in the stadium. This meant that the building and concourse could be smaller, as could the stadium itself, which helped to reduce costs and speed up the programme.

Another positive effect of this design was that the spectators were closer to the athletes and the action than at previous Olympics. This created a good atmosphere.

Team Stadium wanted to limit the amount of material that was transported away from the site. By using good teamwork, challenging ideas and communicating with the contractor before work started on creating the concrete bowl, the team were able to reduce the amount of soil that had to be removed from the ground. They did this by achieving optimum levels, so that the bowl for the permanent seating was partly buried into a slope of the site. This also made it as compact as possible.

The principle of good teamwork was applied throughout the 2012 London Olympic stadium build, including that for the sunken bowl element. Team Stadium, made up of architects, engineers and the building contractor, worked together in this design and build environment. They tested theories and challenged methods as a team, asking key questions to work out whether their ideas would have the right effect and meet the goals of sustainability and legacy.

With a traditional contract, an architect will often go through the whole design process alone and present it to the client. The client then goes out to tender and brings in a contractor, who questions the original design and calls for changes to be made. This, of course, causes delays. Taking Team Stadium's approach of challenging and questioning as an ongoing process helps speed up the building programme. This is because you have already gone through many of what they call the buildability issues by getting the contractor's input at the design stage. Of course, the architect and the engineer can then incorporate that into the design to make it easier and quicker to build.

The upper tiers

The 55,000 temporary seats in the upper tiers were made from steel raking members and precast concrete seating tiers. The steel members were designed with bolted connections to make it easier to take them down later. This took forward the sustainability and legacy ideals of the design team.

The seating bowl, the upper tiers and the roof not only looked like separate elements but also were designed and constructed separately, which helped keep to the timescales of the programme. By separating the lower and upper seating with a clear line, one part of the team was able to design the lower permanent seating while the other part designed the upper seating. They had to communicate with each other throughout because there was an interface between the various elements, but it still helped speed up the programme.

Team Stadium's approach to the upper tiers was homogenous and simple, yet elegant. It was not as grand as the Beijing stadium, but it had its own distinct style. By creating an ethos of good teamwork, Team Stadium showed how using the strengths of their team effectively and sharing out the work in clever ways sped up the design programme.

Sustainability and legacy

Team Stadium also chose to 'embrace the temporary' – a mantra used by the team throughout the build. They wanted to move away from disliking the fact that a large portion of the stadium was going to be temporary and, instead, welcomed it and used it to their advantage.

Robert McAlpine, the main contractor, worked with their subcontractor, Tarmac, to make sure the stadium's precast seating terraces contained as much recycled material as possible. This resulted in 7.5-metre planks that included 30% recycled aggregate in the precast concrete. Taking waste material from one project and using it in another helped to reduce carbon emissions and meet the sustainability goals.

Although this approach has been used in other projects, it is often difficult to identify the materials early enough to include them in the design and to be sure the material will still be available when you need it. But Team Stadium knew that sustainability was one of their key goals. By applying the principle of good teamwork, pooling their

View of stadium showing roof structure supported by diagonal bracing columns painted white.

knowledge and experience to come up with ideal solutions, they were able to identify the waste material early, crush it and store it ready to use in the precast concrete elements.

The roof

The designers wanted a lightweight solution for the roof, so they discussed this with the architects and the engineers. The engineers used computational fluid dynamic modelling and wind-tunnel testing to work out how much roof cover they needed to keep the wind on the track to an acceptable speed. The final design for the cable roof meant that about two-thirds of spectators would be under cover. They developed a fabric cover for the roof, which was supported by a compression ring around the stadium. Radial cables were tied to an inner tension ring – similar to a bicycle wheel on its side.

The compression ring used high-yield large-diameter pipes that had been left over from a North Sea gas pipeline project, helping to meet the sustainability goals. Watson Steel Structures, the steelwork subcontractor, brought the pipes to the attention of Team Stadium and asked if they could use them in the project, thus demonstrating good teamwork. Together, the designers and engineers amended the design to take account of this material.

The pipes were bigger than the ones that the engineers had designed, but the architects said the size was acceptable. They did not change the look of the stadium dramatically, and meeting sustainability goals was important. It also helped speed up the programme and reduce costs – because the pipes were surplus, they cost much less than if they had been new.

This shows that by creating the right environment, everyone in the team can bring ideas like this to the table and get involved in finding the right solution for the project. All the team members feel comfortable to bounce ideas off each other and have an open, honest conversation about what will and won't work. When this sort of teamwork is in place, great things happen and fantastic solutions can be found, even for the most difficult problems.

The lighting towers

The fourteen lighting towers were supported by the cable stay roof. Altogether, they contained 532 individual 2-kilowatt floodlights. The towers were fitted with additional ceremony lighting during the Games, and four of them held large temporary video screens.

The lighting towers had to be adaptable, as events would be held day and night and there were certain requirements for television and athletic events. The team also had to put in extra lighting for the opening and closing ceremonies, even though no one knew what Danny Boyle was going to plan because he had not yet been appointed as director.

Team Stadium had to think ahead, looking at the solutions and methods that other Olympic venues had used. They had to learn from these experiences and use them to make decisions. This demonstrated good team work as they worked together to come up with the best solutions based on the information they had at the time.

As not all of the spectators could see the track close up, Team Stadium wanted to include large television screens (similar to those used at big football and rugby matches) to give live coverage, show replays of events and display the results and photo finishes for people who were further away from the action.

To accommodate television coverage, the stadium lighting needed to be as even as possible and meet the needs of the broadcasters and competitors. The lighting had to be at the right levels for track and field events in all weather and daylight conditions.

The fabric wrap

Controversially, the fabric wrap was funded by DOW Chemical Company, an American company that made the material. Although this saved money, in return DOW wanted to advertise on the wrap during the lead-up to the Olympics. The Olympic Committee are strict about advertising, and they required all sponsor advertising to be agreed in advance and include the London Olympic brand. In an unusual decision, the committee agreed that DOW could advertise the use of its material until 26 June 2012. From then on, the advertising would change solely to the London 2012 branding.

View of steelwork supporting lighting towers

Polyester and polyethylene were used to make the individual sections of the wrap and they were printed with ultraviolet curable ink. The individual sections of the wrap were 2.5 metres wide and twisted at 90-degree angles to allow people to enter the stadium at the bottom of the structure. They were held in place by tension cables.

Leaders create great teams

The architect, Populous, took the role of leading Team Stadium throughout the project design. Populous created the right atmosphere for developing creative solutions to all the problems brought to the table. The architect knew what was required and, with strong leadership, enabled other members of the team to feel confident to challenge ideas and offer solutions, as long as they were tested against the common goals of sustainability and legacy.

A good leader gets the best out of their team but is open to suggestions and ideas. They take responsibility, when necessary, for making difficult decisions. Open communication is key to creating this environment.

We also need to be great leaders in our own businesses. We may not all have a large team to support us, as was the case with Team Stadium, but even as small practices or sole practitioners we need to show leadership qualities if we are to lead our clients.

Clients want to know their options, risks and outlooks. They want you to give them clear, plain and simple information, not jargon or fancy words, so they can make informed decisions. One aspect of leadership involves developing the options, understanding the risks and predicting the outcomes.

Sometimes a solution is more expensive, but it may be the better option because it has more long-term benefits – more flexibility or a longer life, for example. Flexibility is one of the key elements in design today because, as we know, building evolves over time. For example, people now want open-plan living, whereas in the past things were more segregated. You need to use all your experience, knowledge and leadership skills to help your client make the right decisions to meet their goals. You have to discuss the implications of their decisions with them so that they fully understand the consequences of those choices.

Lessons learned

You can become the leader of a great team by creating an ethos of open communication, encouraging respectful challenge and enabling team members to actively engage in problem solving to reach the common goal. To achieve this, you will need to do the following:

1   **Know the strengths and weaknesses of each team member.** This will tell you which parts of the project they are best suited for. You can then play to their strengths. If you know their weaknesses, you can make sure another team member is there to fill that gap.

As much as we like to think that we are very experienced and know a lot, we all have areas for improvement. Play to your team members' strengths and make sure that each person's weaknesses are covered by someone else.

2 **Understand the common goal.** Know what the goal is and take time to explain it to the team and get their buy-in. If the team have not bought into the common goal then you are really on the back foot.

3 **Encourage clear, honest communication** among the whole team and recognise the value of everyone's contribution. No one knows everything, no matter how much experience they have in the industry. By bringing in someone else and asking for their advice, you may see something differently and come up with a fresh alternative. The best solution can be reached by using the strengths of the team members.

By following this key principle of good teamwork, you will get the best from your team members, produce a better outcome for your client and build your reputation and business success.

CHAPTER 5
CREATE A LEGACY IN STONE

Architecture should speak of its time and place, but yearn for timelessness.

Frank Gehry

The importance of legacy

The concept of leaving a lasting legacy for future generations was central to the bid for the London 2012 Olympic Games. In fact, Lord Coe said of the bid at the annual conference of the Central Council of Physical Recreation in 2006 that 'legacy is probably nine-tenths of what this process is about, not just seventeen days of Olympic sport'.

This legacy ran through the very fabric of the Olympic stadium. From the start, the stadium was designed to ensure that it could be enjoyed by people long after the Games had finished.

While it is easy to see the legacy connected with the Olympic stadium, it is not as simple to see the role that legacy plays in smaller building projects. Indeed, some may say that legacy does not play a role in building new houses, adding extensions or other building projects of a smaller stature.

But legacy does feature in every building an architect or engineer is involved in, either consciously or unconsciously, no matter what size it is. When you consciously think about the legacy you want to leave behind with a particular building, it will affect how you feel about the design you are creating and influence that design. It will increase your drive to complete the project in a way that meets that legacy goal.

Legacy is long term, so the fifth principle of running a successful project is to decide what legacy your project will leave from the outset.

PRINCIPLE 5: DECIDE ON THE LEGACY FROM THE OUTSET

The meaning of legacy

1   Legacy means leaving behind something that is noteworthy, of value to others and recognisable. For example, an architect might use a particular style or material. They might be known for designs with sharp edges or cantilevers or use a lot of glass in their buildings.

2   Legacy is about style and the value this gives to the project. An architect wants to build something different – something that will stand out and be noticed. They don't want to create a mundane design.

3   From an engineering perspective, legacy can be about new ways of doing things that may reduce costs, add value and consider how the building will be used in future. Sometimes this means giving clients something they weren't expecting.

Legacy, therefore, is important to the professional and the client, regardless of the size of the project. As a professional you want to leave something behind that is valued by your client or the community. You want to know that you have built something that enhances their life in some way and meets their goals.

Legacy, to the architect or engineer, means:

- innovation
- being different
- achievement
- doing things in an unusual way.

But to your client, legacy means having:

- a better lifestyle
- something to be proud of
- a sense of achievement
- something they can leave to future generations.

Your client will spend a lot of money with you. Leaving them with a building that gives them something they value is creating a legacy.

In this chapter, I focus on how the concept of legacy affected the design and building of the London 2012 Olympic stadium. Legacy drew Team Stadium together as they worked to design and build a stadium that would be flexible enough to not only meet the demands of the 2012 Olympic Games but also serve the community for years to come.

In previous chapters I have dealt with the architecture of the London Olympic scheme. In this chapter I look at the detailed structural design and the role of third-party checkers in achieving the legacy goal. I also look at how you can implement this important principle in your own work.

Detail of the structural design

The island site surrounded by rivers and canals created challenges for the engineers as well as the architect. The stadium had to be designed in a way that made construction easy and met the needs of the wide range of groups who would use the stadium during the Olympics and in the future.

The team wanted everyone to be able to use the stadium with dignity, so the engineers had to ensure that the stadium would meet Paralympians' needs just as much as those of able-bodied athletes attending events. This also applied to disabled and non-disabled spectators.

This meant the engineers had to think creatively about how to implement the design. For example, the slopes that they incorporated into the design of the stadium and the podium could not have a gradient of more than 1:60. To be sure of this, the engineers had to look at the levels during the cut-and-fill process to find the most cost-effective and practical solution across the site.

In previous chapters I have talked about the excavation that was needed to construct the sunken permanent seating bowl. This meant that the podium level was at the top of the permanent seating. The 55,000 temporary seats started at podium level and went upwards, leaving the area below the podium level free for the athletes' facilities (for example, changing rooms and a warm-up track).

The team set the lowest level of the soil so that it was above the groundwater level. An allowance was made for climate change to prevent water coming up through the soil and causing problems with the stadium later.

The engineers then converted the architectural design into engineering elements. That meant they had to work out how some typical sections through the stadium would be designed and constructed while being aware of the changing slope of the soil.

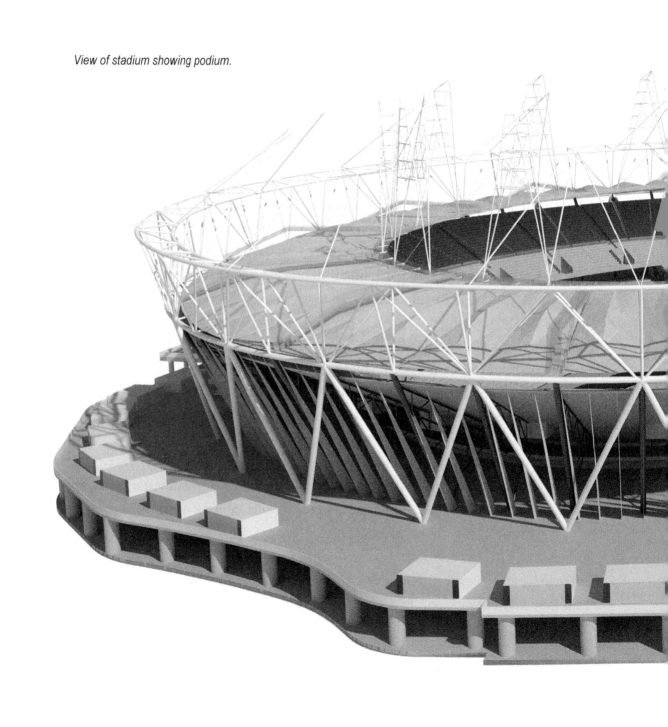

View of stadium showing podium.

Coming up with some typical sections through the stadium allowed them to organise the structural elements in a logical and practical way and design the best solution.

When the engineers built up the level of the soil in layers, they had to consider where the track was going to be in the centre of the stadium and build that up. They had to make sure that the soil could take heavy loads, as a lot of the stadium would need to be built using cranes in the centre. This had to be taken on board early to ensure that the soil was in place before they built all the precast seating.

The podium

The podium is a suspended reinforced concrete structure. It is made of precast concrete supported on ground-bearing reinforced concrete elements. The suspended portion of the podium is a conventional construction. One of the innovative solutions Team Stadium used was to give all the team access to electronic 3D information so that the reinforcement specialists could make the reinforcement cages that were needed, weld them together and bring them to the site.

This planning ahead reduced the time taken to fix the reinforcement cages and controlled tolerances, shortening the length of the construction programme. The concrete podium slab and lower tier were supported on 4,500 reinforced concrete columns on piles, some of which were 20 metres deep. To help reduce carbon for the whole Olympic Park, on-site concrete-batching plants supplied low-carbon concrete to all the contractors who worked on the site.

The original brief called for the structures above podium level to be demountable, so the team came up with a lightweight solution for the steel that would support the upper terrace. They took the Meccano approach, using bolted connections so that after the Games they could easily undo them to take down the portion of the stadium that had the 55,000 temporary seats. This was, of course, key to achieving the legacy goals of the London 2012 bid. It also helped with sustainability, because that portion of the structure could be moved somewhere else and used again.

The upper tier

The contribution of the steel fabricator was important in setting out how the temporary seating would be supported for the upper tier. The steel fabricators wanted as much repetition as possible of the components so they could make and erect them more efficiently. This is why the team chose an oval shape instead of an ellipse shape, as an oval has only three curvatures, while an ellipse has a continuously variable curvature. These contributions helped speed up the programme as well.

The designers gave the steel fabricators the overall geometry of the structural steelwork by using 3D models, with no need to provide detailed dimensions on the drawings. Passing electronic information from one part of the stadium team to the other sped things up. It also improved accuracy by removing some of the human error that could have been a problem.

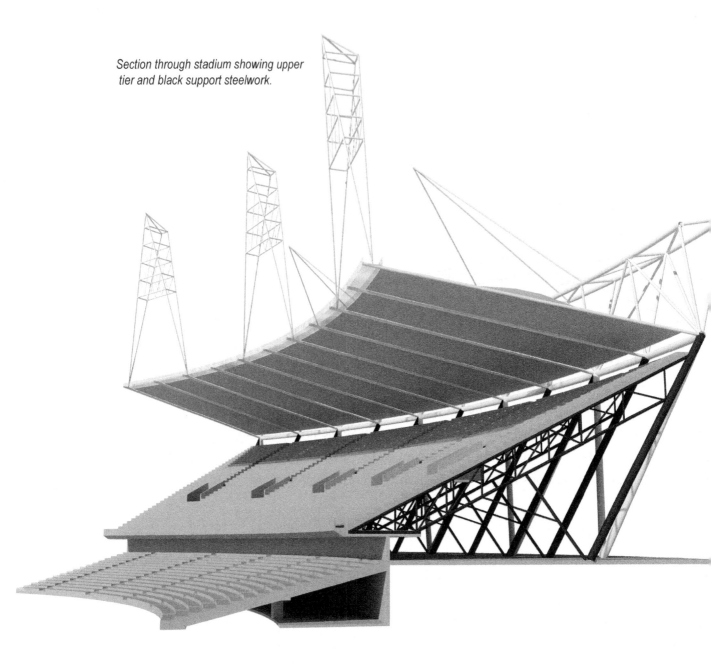

Section through stadium showing upper
tier and black support steelwork.

As discussed in previous chapters, the architect moved all the food outlets out of the stadium onto the podium. This reduced the fire load for the upper tier, so the team did not have to add as much fire protection to the steelwork, again saving time and money and making it possible to do more of the construction on site.

The fire engineers used first principles to design the required fire protection to the steelwork, which resulted in less protection being needed. Because less fire protection was needed, the team could give the steel a clean look. They painted the steel black, because this was the look that the architect wanted – it became known as black steel within Team Stadium. With the steel painted black it became almost invisible underneath the structure, contrasting with the white steelwork of the roof and the sloping columns.

A key engineering innovation was the approach to the dynamic analysis (analysis related to the inertia forces developed by a structure when it is excited by means of dynamic loads applied suddenly) for the upper tier. Usually, when a dynamic load (moving loads such as an excited crowd jumping up and down during part of a sports event or a crowd moving in time to music at a concert) is designed for spectator structures, the engineers want to have a natural frequency above 6 hertz. This approach is now thought to be quite conservative.

The Olympic stadium engineers studied their own data of acceleration analysis and other published data. They took account of different probability functions and

View of roof structure supporting lighting towers.

different event-loading situations and looked at what could happen for the different kinds of events that might be held in the stadium. They then came up with an engineered solution with a much lower frequency. Once it was installed, they did acceleration dynamic tests on the structure and found it confirmed their analysis. With this new approach, the result was a much lighter, more elegant support structure. This contributed to the legacy of the engineers, as it could be used for the design of future sports stadiums.

This all showed how Team Stadium supported the legacy goal. The engineers used their specialists in different areas and agreed concepts with the client and architect up front which enhanced the legacy goal. They used their strengths to come up with innovative designs to leave a lasting legacy with the stadium.

The wrap structure

I have discussed the wrap in previous chapters from an architectural perspective. In this chapter, I deal with the engineer's role in the structure. The engineers supported the wrap structure with steel cables that were attached to the compression ring at the top. The cables were anchored to piled foundations in the ground. These cables were tensioned and the fabric was spanned between them. The team looked at different types of fabric that could span horizontally or vertically.

The engineers decided on eight full-sized prototype panels, which they erected on site and then tested to investigate the advantages of the different types. They looked at how the fabric performed in strong winds, as they did not want it to have too much flutter in windy conditions. By testing these full-size prototypes, they could combine the good points from all them to arrive at the best solution.

With a project of this size, the team could afford to build the prototypes. The engineers and the contractor built this into the programme at the design and construction stage so they had enough time to build the prototypes, test them and come up with the best solution.

The roof

The team designed the roof to be temporary and lightweight. As mentioned before, they looked at the cantilever option but settled on the 'bicycle wheel' design, which had a compression ring on the outside and a tension ring on the inside, with cables in between. The fabric that covered two-thirds of the roof was then spanned across the cables and cut into separate panels to prevent creases in the roof. Team Stadium used engineers with specialist knowledge of fabric roofs, an example of using the right specialists in the right areas.

Part of the roof design needed to support the sports lighting for the Olympic events. The team also had to consider the lighting that would be needed for the opening and closing ceremonies. The lighting needed to be temporary, as it had to be removed after the Games. The sports lights had to be supported on the roof so they could light up the Games and support the use of high-definition television, as the Games would be broadcast around the world. The total power required for the lights was more than 1 megawatt. The correct lighting angles had to be used from the track and field, as very low angles would dazzle the spectators and athletes. The lights had to be between 30 metres and 42 metres above the roof covering, and were 12 metres high and were supported on the tension ring. They were then tied back to the compression ring with tension cables.

The roof support

As mentioned previously, the team had to take account of what might happen during the opening and closing ceremonies when designing the roof support. Based on their research, they developed a brief for the likely loading and layout. This resulted in two sets of rigging – the first to support the lighting and the second to support the moving people and equipment that would use the 3D space of the stage set. This increased the complexity of the design of the roof structure. The roof support design complied with the legacy ideals as it was temporary and would be removed after the games.

The role of the third-party checker

The main role of the third-party checker during the 2012 stadium design and build was to ensure that the stadium would stand up and that it was fit for purpose. It was their job to question and challenge assumptions and designs.

Third-party checkers work on the basis that they would rather ask too many questions and have them answered 'yes' than not ask enough and miss a vital piece of information. This is not meant to disrespect the engineers' skills and experience, but it is crucial that the third-party checker understand why the engineers choose to do something in the way they do.

The third-party checkers were not part of Team Stadium, so they needed to develop a good relationship with the relevant people (their counterparts and specialists on the engineering side of Team Stadium) so they could question, challenge and find the information they needed easily.

There were also third-party checkers for the architectural, mechanical and electrical elements of the stadium. The checkers communicated with each other to ensure they covered everything.

Third-party checkers, by the nature of their questioning role, need to be at a distance from the rest of the design and construction team. This was the case with the London 2012 stadium project. The third-party checkers were given the drawings of the design, but they were not given the teams' calculations or loads. This was because they needed to do their own independent calculations, put their own checks in place and be sure that the Olympic stadium would fulfil its purpose. They had to be sure that the stadium would not have any major issues and that the client, the ODA, was getting value for money and achieving its goals.

The third-party checkers had a key role in ensuring that the 2012 Olympics would leave a legacy. They made sure that the Olympic stadium would stand up and helped Team Stadium meet the goal that it would meet the needs of the generations to come.

Resourcing third-party checkers

Various specialists were brought in to support this aspect of the work. For example, there were specialists in fabric canopies and tension fabrics, in precast concrete, in vibration and in 3D geometry, and in drawing and setting out. Specialists also helped to make models of the stadium, which were used to analyse the stadium and its parts.

Everyone on the third-party checking team had to have good communication skills, be diplomatic and be solution-focused – it was crucial to solve problems on paper, before they had a chance to appear on site.

Lessons learned

To leave a lasting legacy, regardless of the size of your building project, you will need to take the following steps:

1   Understand all the detail (including the legacy goal) in the brief and challenge the client so that you understand what they want and why.

2   Decide on the legacy right from the start. Include the team in this so they buy into the goal from the beginning.

3 Incorporate your client's vision and drivers for their legacy into the design.

4 Have the right team in place so team members work together to create this legacy.

5 Complete a project that can be used for the purpose it was intended for. Tessa Jowell, then Secretary of State for Culture, Media and Sport, said:

> *You host them [The Games] because of the power of the legacy and the great national moment that hosting a Games creates... the power of government to back something that was going to be transformational to east London but also to all those kids with unfulfilled potential, up and down the country, who love their sport, and if anything was going to harness that, it was an Olympic Games.*

The concept of the legacy had to be planned for, and part of that planning was to create a vision for the future, beyond the Games themselves. You can adapt and use this model of thinking in your own programmes and visions for the projects you are working on in your business.

CHAPTER 6
WILL IT STAND UP?

If a surgeon makes a mistake, he could kill a patient. If an
engineer makes a mistake, he could kill thousands.
Unknown

The importance of checking procedures

Construction mistakes cost money – lots of money. Mistakes could also cost lives, so safety procedures ought to be high on your agenda. Never assume that people are safe. All construction areas must have solid systems for checking safety before the building starts.

At its worst, without the correct checking procedures in place you will run the risk of litigation and reputational damage. This is why having a robust process for checking forms our sixth principle of running a successful project.

PRINCIPLE 6:
DEVELOP ROBUST CHECKING PROCEDURES BEFORE YOU START

In the previous chapter I talked about the third-party checker's role in helping Team Stadium meet the legacy goal for the London 2012 Olympics. In this chapter, I discuss why checking is so important on any building project, when checking should start and what types of checks you need to do throughout the life of the project. I look at the construction of the London Olympic stadium in detail and the checking procedures that took place during this time.

Start from the beginning

Checking should start at the beginning of a project. Check that from day one you have all your client's contact details – at least their email address and phone number. This standard information is often forgotten, showing a lack of professionalism right from the start of the relationship with the client.

After gathering the client's contact information, you should carry out checks at the following stages of the building project:

- After the first site visit, save photographs and scan all hand-written documents, on-site observations or comments and sketches, and other information and download them to a server. It is essential to store all this information safely while ensuring that the whole team have access to it when they need it. By having all of this information readily available, any aspects of the site visit or construction at that time can be checked quickly and easily, and can help resolve any issues before they become a major problem.

- Once the design has been done, check it. Work out the loads to ensure they are correct. If you get these right, everything else will follow.

- When mock-ups have been done, it is vital to check them to make sure they are accurate. With computer-aided drafting (CAD), drawings can be created from the design and sent to the engineer for checking. In this checking phase, examine all the different elements on the drawing, from the client's name to the beam sizes, steel grades and connections.

- The final check of the design and calculations is carried out by an independent checker. Often a different engineer will check the design engineer's work – this makes sure you can highlight any issues that have been missed as a priority.

- Finally, once on site, the contractor will do their own checks. These include checking the dimensions to ensure that the drawings reflect what is actually on site.

My team was contracted as the third-party checker for the engineering and technical review of the London 2012 Olympic stadium. It was our role to ensure that the design and stadium were safe for the public to use.

Building the Olympic stadium

On 13 October 2006, the London Organising Committee confirmed that it had selected Sir Robert McAlpine as the main contractor, Populous as the architect, and BuroHappold as the engineers to design and build the Olympic stadium. The stadium design was launched on 7 November 2007. The initial land preparation for the stadium began in mid-2007 with an official construction start date of 22 May 2008, although piling works for the foundations began four weeks earlier.

On 29 March 2011, Rod Sheard, Senior Principal Architect at Populous, said:

> *The construction of the world's most environmentally friendly Olympic Stadium has taken just over 1,000 days, in the world of major construction, this could be considered as a sprint, its completion marked the beginning of the end of the construction phase of London's Olympic Games. We can now all look forward to just under 500 days of the final preparation to when the world will see this innovative design performed for the first time.*

As has been said, because Team Stadium was effectively an integrated design team made up of the contractor, architect, engineer and client, they could have open discussions on site, which resulted in fewer delays throughout the project. And because of this constant contact, they were able to manage each other's expectations of what needed to be done while managing the client's expectations too.

The architect, Populous, also helped to manage public expectations by issuing visuals of the stadium and keeping the media up to speed on the design and build. This helped to reduce the risk of big disappointments later.

On-site observations

The concrete podium slabs that formed the public-access level were supported on more than 4,500 reinforced concrete columns on piles up to 20 metres deep. The contractor checked the planned position and level of the piles to ensure that they would be installed in the correct place.

An on-site concrete-batching plant was set up to supply low-carbon concrete to all the contractors working on the Olympic venues. This reduced the embodied carbon (the carbon dioxide emitted during the manufacture, transport and construction of building materials, such as concrete, together with end of life emissions) associated with the site as a whole, helping to meet sustainability goals.

While the compression truss and roof columns were being erected, Team Stadium carried out continuous surveys to check the tolerances and the corresponding steel temperature so they could be sure that the compression truss would continue to fit even when the steel heated up and expanded. They measured the temperature during each survey, so that they could compare the survey results and calibrate them with the results of the theoretical analysis.

This attention to detail meant that the whole compression truss was erected and assembled without the need for any steel packs. This showed that the checks done by Team Stadium improved the build of the stadium.

After the tensioning net had been lifted in to the air, the cable net was erected. From their analysis, the fabricator and the engineer had worked out that detailed prescribed checks would be needed so that the cable net could be gradually lifted further into the air. The engineers wrote bespoke software to meet the geometrical requirements at each stage of the checking process. From this analysis, they were able to calculate the distribution of cable forces to allow a perfectly vertical lift at each of the tensioning nodes without affecting the position of the rest of the nodes. The team then confirmed these results by comparing them with the main analysis model.

One of the final checks needed was to verify the geometry of the roof and the lighting towers once they had been erected. This was done using a full 3D laser scan of the entire stadium structure. This technology enabled the team to check the information they had analysed against the design to make sure that the roof and towers would be safe. This showed that the checks done by Team Stadium improved the build of the stadium.

The subcontractor's input

The programme was extremely tight, with only six and a half months from finishing the concept design to beginning the piling on site. Procuring the structural steelwork early was critical. The structural steel subcontractor, Watson Steel Structures, supplied 10,600 tonnes of structural steelwork for the stadium. To meet sustainability criteria, 34% of the steel and concrete in the stadium was recycled. The stadium was built using less than half the steel that was used in comparable Olympic stadiums, which reduced the effect on the environment and made it the lightest Olympic stadium to be constructed at that time.

As mentioned earlier, to help meet the sustainability criteria, Watson suggested using steel tubes left over from the North Sea gas pipeline project in Russia. These tubes were slightly wider in diameter and shorter than those proposed by the structural engineers, but the engineers adapted the design accordingly. The roof also used 52 tonnes of scrap metal, some of which was from keys, knives and guns that had been confiscated by London's Metropolitan Police. In this way, it was possible to use less than a quarter of the steel that was used for the Beijing stadium in 2008.

View of inside of stadium showing seating tiers and roof.

The main contractor, Sir Robert McAlpine, worked with their subcontractor, Tarmac, to make sure the seating terraces contained as much recycled material as possible. The precast concrete planks included 30% recycled aggregate made from crushed concrete, again meeting the sustainability goal. The continuous checks against the sustainability criteria ensured that the sustainability goals were met.

Practicalities and ease of installation

As an integrated design team, Team Stadium were able to incorporate practicalities and ease of installation into the design early on. Having the contractor in the team from the start made it possible to check issues relating to buildability and installation in the original design.

A similar integrated team approach was taken to building Ipswich Town Football Club's North Stand, which was one of my projects. To make sure the separate parts fitted and aligned as intended, the main shear walls were match-cast in pairs, with the steel shoe connectors placed at the mid-height of the pair. The shoes were then welded together on site. To make sure the connections between the steel beams and the shear walls were accurate, the fittings had to be installed on the walls with special care. At the start of the design process for the North Stand, it became obvious that the qualities of manufacture and tolerance control were critical to erecting the stand as required on site. Because of the complexity of the interfaces between the precast elements and the steelwork, close co-ordination was needed between the suppliers and the erection crew on site. This meant that the supply and erection of the entire structure should form one package.

This strategy proved to be the right one to take, as not a single unit failed to fit when it was assembled on site. Because the entire package was negotiated on an open-book basis, the contractor could give specialist advice early in the design process yet the client and architect could still be flexible about which type of concrete to choose during negotiations on price. This means of procurement achieved many of the ideals set out in the Egan report on better construction practice, including manufacturing as much as possible away from the site.

The award by negotiation on an open-book basis (the method of procuring work under which contractors are reimbursed on the basis of transparent records of the costs they have incurred) throughout the supply chain, combined with good communication, openness and a shared desire to solve technical and logistical problems quickly to achieve the common goal, resulted in a successful project.

This is another example of the effectiveness of using the integrated design team approach taken by Team Stadium from the start of the London 2012 project. This showed that continuous checks were done to ensure that the stadium progressed satisfactorily and was a success.

Bolting

Because large sections of the Olympic stadium had to be temporary, the roof was designed to be structurally independent from the terrace. A 900-metre compression ring truss formed the roof and was supported on inclined tubular columns. Because the structure needed to be demountable, all the site connections, including those between the steel and the precast concrete, had to be designed and made as bolted connections. This included those to the roof and to the sloping rakers that supported the 55,000 temporary seats on the upper tier.

None of the connections were welded. This shows that right from the beginning, before they had even started building the stadium, Team Stadium were planning ahead to make it easy to dismantle the roof and seating. These checks early on in the design process ensured that the legacy goals were met.

Superstructure of the stadium bowl

The precast concrete terrace units for the sunken stadium bowl, which supported the 25,000 permanent seats, were supported on concrete rakers. These rakers were supported on around 4,500 columns on piles.

The concrete piers on the podium support 123 steel raker beams, which carry the precast concrete terrace units for the 55,000 temporary seats in the upper tiers. Everything below the seating terraces was painted black, including the steelwork and

View of black steelwork supporting upper terraces.

the electrical and mechanical services. The steel raker beams were I-beam sections and were bolted together, with all the connections on show. Taking an innovative approach, the team used pre-welded, pre-fixed reinforcement cages for the suspended slab beams and columns for the upper tier. This meant that these large reinforcement cages were welded together before arriving at the stadium and then craned into position as one big unit when they arrived.

The engineers, the main contractor and the subcontractor worked closely to provide the required information in 3D. This reduced the fixing time on site, saving time on the overall installation programme. It also helped control the tolerances, because they were given by the pre-welded cages. The quality-control and checking procedures could be done before the cages arrived at the site.

The roof girders were made as large as possible, but there were limits because they had to be transported easily. The girders were made and assembled as much as possible at the factory so the team could bring them to the site just in time to lift them into position.

Team Stadium included as few components as possible in the design, which allowed them to use simple connections. This reduced the build time on site, the amount of checking needed and the overall length of the construction programme.

Close up view of roofing structure and lighting tower.

The roof structure

The roof cover was made from PVC fabric. As mentioned earlier, it was supported on the cable net with an inner cable ring and an outer steel compression truss. The compression truss was 900 metres long and 12 metres deep, supported at 32 positions by inclined raking tubular columns down to ground level. These are the sloping white columns that are so distinctive around the perimeter of the stadium. The team used simple flange connections to bolt the compression truss, making it easy to assemble and dismantle. Individual sections of the ring truss were faceted rather than curved, which reduced the fabrication costs.

Ten 60-millimetre-diameter cables formed the inner cable tension ring, which were connected by steel brackets at 6-metre centres. These supported the continuous walkway. Individual parts of the ring truss were delivered to the central area and assembled in 30-metre sections that weighed about 100 tonnes each.

The team had to support the truss on temporary works from the terrace structure until the whole truss was complete. When it was all connected together, the truss was stable and the team could remove the temporary support work.

A temporary platform was built at terrace level so the team could assemble the cable tension ring at a low level. They fixed the tie-down and suspension cables to the compression truss at a high level and laid it out across the terrace using temporary mats to prevent damage to the precast units or the cables. They fixed temporary pulling cables to the ends of the suspension cable, completing the inner ring. They attached the pulling cables to the thirty-two separate strand jacks at the top of the tension ring.

Erecting the lighting towers was extremely challenging. This was partly because of the weight and the lifting radius, and partly because the towers were not stable until the final high-level circumferential cable had been connected and pre-stressed. All fourteen of the lighting towers were fully assembled and fitted out at ground level before they were lifted into place by a 600-tonne capacity crawler crane.

As explained previously, the compression truss was connected to a central hub with tension members. It had an inner tension ring of ten steel cables instead of a hub, which created a central opening. The team used temporary scaffolding while assembling the cable ring. They then raised the cable ring by slowly pulling the cables connecting it to the outer truss with jacks.

As mentioned before, a 12-metre-high truss forms the outer ring. This was made in twenty-eight sections, each of which was 30 metres long. To make sure it fitted together as it should, the team measured the last piece on site before it was made. This allowed for the steelwork to expand in warmer temperatures, overcame any manufacturing and installation errors and created a tight fit. This showed again that the checks that Team Stadium did enhanced the build of the stadium.

On 20 December 2010, the Prime Minister David Cameron attended an exclusive ceremony in the stadium to officially turn the lights on. The symbolism of the date was no coincidence. As 20 December spells out 2012, it was a key landmark in the construction process.

Identifying problems and solutions

Having the contractor in the team from the start meant that the engineers could discuss how the stadium was going to be built from the beginning and incorporate everything needed for the erection in the initial design. The main contractor and steel fabricator worked with the engineers to carry out a fully integrated appraisal of all aspects of erecting the stadium.

The cable-net design reduced the number of temporary works as far as possible, but some were still needed in the bowl structure. The team incorporated these into the original design so that when they were needed, they were already in place.

The level of detail, preparation and co-ordination by everyone involved meant that the team could include all the temporary works in the bowl structure as it was being built. Team Stadium recognised that erecting the lighting towers would be complicated, so they carried out a staged analysis for each tower. This included checking that the wind load would be no higher than the loads in the permanent design while the lighting towers were being installed.

Positional monitors were installed on the tension ring, and all the force-monitoring equipment and lighting towers and force-monitoring equipment were installed on several members. To make sure the lighting towers were erected safely, the team compared the data from the monitoring equipment with the results of the analysis. They erected the roof in four weeks, checking continuously that none of the elements were overstressed and could cause any failures.

This detailed checking reflects the experience and skill within Team Stadium. The upper-terrace steel structure was erected on two fronts, working from the south-east corner using crawler cranes.

This was followed closely by installing the precast terrace units using separate tower cranes. The steel contractor installed the precast units to minimise any site clashes. All the units were incorporated into the steelwork model during the detailing stage. These checks ensured that everything fitted as it should on site.

The engineers were very experienced in this kind of design, erection and analysis. They had the right team, with the right specialists in place at the right time to do this work. Because the contractor, Sir Robert McAlpine, had built the Arsenal Stadium with Populous and BuroHappold, they had already formed a good working relationship and knew they could trust each other's judgement.

Team Stadium implemented checking procedures right from the start of the design process. The third-party checkers formed part of this team for the duration of the project. By thinking ahead, working together, planning together and co-ordinating how they could overlap each other's activities, they helped shorten the construction programme, kept costs down, met their target date and ensured that the Olympic stadium would safely fulfil its purpose.

Lessons learned

The working relationships in Team Stadium were enhanced because they were all on site together and they all worked towards the mantra of embracing the temporary. All the checking procedures were done with this in mind. This is not the case with all building projects, though.

You can build an effective relationship with your third-party checker in the following ways:

- **Develop an honest, open relationship** where questions can be asked easily and challenges responded to professionally.

- **Bring them in as part of your team.** You all have the same objective, so use this understanding to build your relationship and achieve your goal successfully together.

- **Make sure you give them all the relevant information up front**, before they start the checking. This will save you time, effort and money.

- **See your third-party checker as a facilitator** who will give the client even more confidence in the project delivery. It is their responsibility to question relevant aspects of the project to ensure that it is a success.

In this chapter I have covered the importance of putting checking procedures in place right from the beginning of the design phase. Using the London 2012 Olympic stadium project as an example, I have discussed the impact this had on making sure the stadium was safe to use and meeting sustainability and legacy goals.

You may not be working on such a large project as the Olympic stadium, but no matter what the size of your project, putting in place checking procedures from the start will prevent major issues occurring later, save you time and money, and build your reputation.

CHAPTER 7
FIT FOR PURPOSE

We lit the flames and we lit up the world. We know more now as individuals and as a nation just what we are capable of. When our time came, Britain, we did it right. Thank you.

Sebastian Coe at the closing ceremony of the 2012 London Olympics

The importance of being fit for purpose

You have finally delivered your project: you have met your client's specification and all their objectives. But it is one thing for your building to look good and come in on budget but it is another to fulfil the function it was designed and built for. If it doesn't do that then it has failed.

This important factor forms our final principle of running a successful project and that is ensuring your building is fit for purpose.

PRINCIPLE 7: MAKE SURE YOUR PROJECT IS FIT FOR PURPOSE

What does fit for purpose mean?

The Olympic stadium had to fulfil many requirements to meet the needs of all the different people who would use it during the 2012 Olympic Games and beyond. Firstly, the stadium had to be able to seat 80,000 people. If it could only seat 60,000, it would have failed because it would not have met the first objective. It also had to host athletics events effectively and safely, which meant having a track with the right number of lanes that kept to international standards. For example, the wind speed on the track had to be controlled to guarantee that any records set were valid. If the team hadn't been aware of all the criteria that would make the stadium fit for purpose from the start, the 2012 Olympics would not have been the success they were.

This principle applies regardless of the size of your project. For example, if you are designing a floor for a project you should consider its strength and safety. You should make sure its natural frequency is above the required limits so that when you walk on it, it doesn't feel too bouncy. When you design a racecourse stand, to make it fit for purpose you have to understand not only its structure and architecture but also how the client is going to use it.

NRM Bobrowski designed the Centaur Building, a multi-purpose sports arena for Cheltenham Racecourse. This was one of my projects. As part of the design, the team had to consider the types of events that might be hosted there. These ranged from indoor basketball to indoor tennis, and from indoor show jumping to rock concerts and car shows. To accommodate this range of events, my team designed trusses that could carry large temporary loads at certain points so that, for example, for car shows, they could suspend cars from the trusses.

The reason this project was so successful is that we asked the client detailed questions to get a full understanding of what they were going to use the building for and how we could help them achieve that. Being able to hang extra loads from the trusses gave the client much more flexibility in how they used their facility. This meant that they could host a wider variety of events and increase their revenue streams.

The key to ensuring that any building is fit for purpose is to make sure you understand what the client wants to use it for. In doing this you can also help the client see how they might use their new facility more effectively and show them the flexibility of the structure you are building.

When your client knows that their building, regardless of what it is, is designed properly and is going to stand up and fulfil its function, it is fit for purpose. That gives them confidence in the work you have done.

Five steps to fitness for purpose

Following these five steps will help make sure your project is fit for purpose.

1   Understand your client's needs. Ask them questions to get that complete understanding.

2   Challenge yourself and your client by asking if this is going to work or if there is a better way to do it.

3   Test your ideas and then test them again.

4   Evaluate your ideas and decide which you will use.

5   Be flexible and ready to change if new information or new technology suggests a better way.

The Olympic Committee had a long list of strict criteria that the stadium had to meet to be fit for purpose. One of these was that several different types of events had to be able to take place safely at the same time. For example, javelin needed to be held simultaneously with middle-distance events, discus with high jump and hammer-throwing with long jump.

Each area had to be carefully planned so there was no risk of other athletes or spectators being injured. But here, to an extent, Team Stadium had previous experience: having worked on the stadium for the Sydney Olympics, they knew what was needed to deal with these practicalities.

One of the biggest challenges in making the Olympic stadium fit for purpose came when dealing with the unknowns of the opening and closing ceremonies.

The opening and closing ceremonies

Here, the architect and structural engineers had to work in the dark. The director had not been appointed yet, so the requirements for the ceremonies were unknown. How could the team ensure that the Olympic stadium would be fit for purpose on opening night without any information on what might be needed?

To do this, the architect and the structural engineers had to make assumptions about the loads that might be expected for the opening and closing ceremonies. The engineers studied the requirements of previous Olympic opening and closing ceremonies to understand what might be needed for the London 2012 Olympic stadium.

This had to take place many years before Danny Boyle was appointed as director. The ability to carry any additional loads needed to be designed from the outset and included in the structure as the stadium was being built. The team could not wait until the appointed person was in place, as they would not have had enough time to incorporate the requirements into the stadium design so late in the programme. In effect, the engineers defined the practical limits of the opening and closing ceremonies before the event designers arrived.

View of Universities Athletics test event held in May 2012.

Fit for purpose testing

To ensure that the stadium would function as intended, the London Organising Committee organised a series of test events to be held in the stadium in the year before the Olympic Games. These test events were called the London Prepares series.

The first public test event was held on 31 March 2012, where the stadium served as the finish line for the National Lottery Olympic Park Run. Five thousand people took part, including celebrities, British athletes and members of the public who had won a draw organised by the National Lottery to get a place in the run. After taking part in a 5-mile run around the Olympic Park, they entered the Olympic stadium to the theme of 'Chariots of Fire', where they ran the final 300 metres on the athletics track.

Two warm-up events for the London 2012 Olympic and Paralympic Games were held as part of the London Prepares series at the Olympic stadium. They were the British Universities Athletics Championships in early May 2012 and the London Disability Grand Prix held in late May 2012. Four new world records were set during the London Disability Grand Prix.

On 6 May 2012, 40,000 people attended an athletics and entertainment event that was cleverly entitled 2012 Hours To Go. Gabby Logan and Vernon Kay hosted the event, which also included John Culshaw, Mel C, Hugh Bonneville, the Chipmunks and Jack Whitehall. The person who was chosen to open the stadium ceremonially was nine-year-old Niamh Clarke-Willis. The British Games was also hosted in the Olympic stadium as part of this series. These events were powerful testing tools for Team Stadium, enabling them to see whether the stadium was fit for purpose.

The Olympic cauldron

The cauldron that was used for the Olympic flame during the Olympic and Paralympic Games in London 2012 was designed by Thomas Heatherwick. Heatherwick is a prize-winning designer whose previous work includes the Seed Cathedral at the 2010 Shanghai Expo and the new Routemaster bus, which was introduced in London in February 2012. He was chosen by Danny Boyle to design one cauldron to serve both Games. This was a new approach, as in other Olympic Games different cauldrons had been created for the Olympics and Paralympics.

The brief for the cauldron was that it should be something that connected all the nations with the idea of being part of the Games and that it should have a story. The idea was that the cauldron should be placed among the people in the stadium rather than towering over them and being supported in the roof, as had been done in past Olympic Games. Heatherwick wanted the cauldron to be a focal point, like an altar in a church. He described it as 'The coming together in peace of 204 nations for two weeks of sporting competition. A representation of extraordinary, albeit transitory togetherness that the Olympic Games symbolise.'

The cauldron was made up of 204 separate copper petals for the Olympics and 164 petals for the Paralympics – one petal for each of the competing nations.

The cauldron was 8.5 metres high and 8 metres wide when flat on the ground. It weighed 16 tonnes. It was a lot smaller and lighter than those of previous Olympic Games – for example, the cauldron for the Beijing 2008 Summer Olympic Games weighed 300 tonnes. The stems for the petals were formed of stainless steel rods, and the cauldron burned natural gas. It incorporated a variable burn rate so the gas consumption could be reduced to 15% when the stadium was not being used, keeping to the sustainability agenda. The cauldron was given the code name Betty, as there was strict security and secrecy around it during the construction and testing.

The identities of the athletes who would light the cauldron were kept secret too. As the aim was to inspire a generation, seven young people were chosen for that honour. Sir Steve Redgrave carried the flame into the stadium and passed it on to one of the team of six young athletes and one young volunteer, who had each been nominated by a famous British Olympian.

The seven young people stepped forward together to light one petal each. The flames spread radially around the petals, and when all were alight, the stems rose slowly from the floor of the arena and converged to form an upright cauldron with a single massive flame, symbolising 204 nations coming together to form one. The audience in the stadium gasped when the cauldron lifted to form the single great flame.

When it came to the closing ceremony, the operation of the cauldron was played in reverse as it opened out and fell flat on the ground, and then the flames in the petals were extinguished one by one.

At the end of the Paralympic Games, each of the individual petals was removed from the cauldron, cleaned and packaged in presentation boxes that were sent to each country as a souvenir of the London 2012 Olympic Games.

Heatherwick and his team tested the cauldron at the Stage One's workshop, which was screened from the public to keep it secret, and to make sure that everything was fine and that it was fit for purpose. The cauldron was given a final night-time test the day before the opening ceremony to ensure that everything was working. It had to be done at night as the Olympic airspace restrictions were in place to prevent press helicopters from getting a view and maintain the secrecy of the cauldron.

The Olympic torch relay

The Olympic torches attracted a lot of attention from the moment the Olympic flame set off on its 8,000-mile journey from Land's End in Cornwall. The torches were gold coloured and were 800 millimetres high. They had 8,000 perforations to represent the 8,000 torchbearers who would each carry a torch along their leg of the route. The torchbearers were allowed to keep their torch after they had completed their part of the journey.

Derek Mason with the 2012 Olympic torch, together with Ben Hunt-Davis with his Sydney Olympic 2000 gold medal for the men's rowing 8 event.

Some 15 million people had cheered the Olympic torch on its way through more than a thousand communities by the time Sir Steve Redgrave brought the Olympic flame into the opening ceremony. The route for the torch relay went within 10 miles of 95% of the UK population, giving as many people as possible the chance to see it.

When each country's team arrived in London for the Games, they had a welcome ceremony. This was a 30-minute production by the National Youth Theatre, complete with dancers, clowns and jesters. National anthems were played, and each team was invited to sign the Truce Wall, which has been an Olympic tradition since the Sydney Games in 2000 and aims to promote peace through sport. IOC President Jacques Rogge said, 'Sport is not immune from and cannot cure all the ills of the world. But sport can help bridge differences and bring people together. We can see proof of that at these games.'

Safety of the Games

The Olympic Games was the biggest event staged in this country in peacetime. Nevertheless, it meant making the most extensive security arrangements, and both IOC President Jacques Rogge and Prime Minister David Cameron stressed that the safety of the athletes and the public was the top priority. Although it wasn't up to Team Stadium to manage security arrangements, they needed to design a stadium in which the safety of the public and athletes could be managed as effectively as possible. For example, the main security lines were the five bridges that allowed the spectators to enter the stadium on the island site.

Because of the global scale of the Olympic and Paralympic Games, the success of both events relied heavily on the technology involved, both in managing individual competitions and delivering them to spectators and the media.

A state-of-the-art communication system was provided by sponsors and partners. This required 350 technologists to keep 950 servers and 16,000 desktops, notebooks and tablets running twenty-four hours a day, seven days a week throughout the Olympic and Paralympic Games. This communications network, which could have serviced a small city, was controlled and kept running smoothly from the Technology Operations Centre in Olympic Park.

Complex systems like this have to be almost unbreakable and be secure against cyber threats to make them fit for purpose. The team carried out more than 200,000 hours of testing, throwing hundreds of different problems at the system and its operators – anything from internet viruses to simple mistakes such as someone pulling a plug out. This thorough testing ensured that all aspects of the stadium, not just the structure, were fit for purpose.

London 2012 introduced one major innovation – the commentator information system (CIS). With the CIS, the 21,000 accredited broadcasters and 6,500 accredited press could see the results of the events in real time. This meant that times and places could sometimes be confirmed before the crowd had even reacted. This showed that London

2012 was fully up to speed with technology and that it was fit for purpose.

The opening ceremony

The job of masterminding the opening ceremony at London 2012 was taken by Danny Boyle as a tribute to his late father, who had ignited his love of the Olympic Games. Bradley Wiggins, the British winner of the Tour de France and triple Olympic champion, rang the largest harmonically tuned bell in the world to signal the start of the opening ceremony in front of a packed Olympic stadium.

The ceremony dazzled hundreds of millions of viewers around the world. It began with a countryside scene of green and pleasant farmland, complete with animals and maypole dancing. This was transformed into an industrial landscape, where thousands of performers re-enacted the country's industrial revolution. A stunt-double of Queen Elizabeth II made a dramatic entrance, parachuting into the stadium with James Bond after being shown flying in a helicopter from Buckingham Palace.

The ceremony paid tribute to Britain's National Health Service and continued the tradition of slapstick humour with a performance by Mr Bean. This was followed by a tribute to the country's musical heritage, which featured 1,400 dancers and music from 1960 to 2012.

This was followed by a parade of nations, which saw athletes from 204 national Olympic committees march into the stadium. After this, Queen Elizabeth II declared the Games officially open. The Olympic torch arrived outside the stadium, where it was handed to Sir Steve Redgrave, the five-time Olympic champion, by David Beckham and a young footballer called Jade Bailey, who arrived by speedboat after travelling along the River Thames.

IOC President Jacques Rogge said during his speech:

> *I congratulate all of the athletes who have earned a place at these games. And to the athletes I offer this thought. Your talent, your dedication and commitment brought you here. Now you have a chance to become true Olympians. That honour is determined not by whether you win, but how you compete. Character counts far more than medals.*

Sebastian Coe said afterwards:

> *The athletes competing at the Olympic Games have arrived in London to give the performance of their lives. We wanted to provide a very British welcome for them and the rest of the world. Danny Boyle has created a show of memories and moments that will last a lifetime for people across the UK and the world.*

The opening ceremony was a huge success, and it showed that the decisions that the stadium designers had made for the loads were the correct ones. They enabled Danny Boyle to put on a spectacular show, proving the stadium was fit for purpose.

The closing ceremony

The closing ceremony was held on 12 August, marking the end of the many impressive sporting achievements that had taken place in the stadium during the Olympic Games. The stadium played host to a colourful ceremony that celebrated the best of British music with performances by artists Annie Lennox, One Direction, the Spice Girls, George Michael, The Who and Take That, among others. When the Olympic flag was lowered, President Rogge paid tribute to the London 2012 volunteers and the enthusiastic support from the fans throughout the Games.

As the Olympic Games would next be hosted by Rio de Janeiro, the London 2012 Olympic stadium was transformed into a Brazilian carnival scene, with samba dancers and an appearance from football legend Pele. As the London 2012 Olympic Games came to a close, the Olympic flame was extinguished. Lord Coe said, 'This may be the end of these two glorious weeks in London, but what we have begun will not stop now. The spirit of these Olympic games will inspire a generation.'

By ensuring that the Olympic stadium was fit for purpose – not only for the opening and closing ceremonies but also for the athletes, spectators, television crews and technology teams, among many others – the ceremonies were a resounding success.

Lessons learned

Regardless of whether you are designing a small or large structure for your client, one of the ultimate goals is for it to be fit for purpose.

As can be seen from the complex needs of the London Olympic stadium, it is vital to fully understand your client's needs and exactly what they want to use the building for. Ask careful questions to get a full understanding of what fit for purpose means for them – this understanding will enable you to achieve that goal.

Challenge your client on the key points to clarify the requirements for you and them. It may also lead your client to see how they could get even more use out of their building.

Test aspects of your project before it is completed. This will tell you whether the structure is truly fit for purpose. Evaluate your results continuously and be ready to make changes that are needed to meet the goal of being fit for purpose. This is why, for example, they tested the cauldron in the workshop to check if everything worked and made adjustments where required, before it was installed in the stadium.

Finally, be flexible. Know when something isn't right and change it. Look for changes in technology that will improve your structure and make use of them. The extensive time testing the communication system ensured that it worked properly and was fit for a wide range of purposes.

CHAPTER 8
BUILD ON SUCCESS

The Olympic Park was another great British success story. A committed workforce sharing a vision, uniting to build something truly special, on time and under budget.

Dennis Hone, Chief Executive of the ODA

The importance of building on success

The London 2012 Olympic Games were a triumph. According to the President of the IOC, London had 'absolutely refreshed the Games... These were athletes' Games, the athletes' village was fantastic, the venues were state of the art and well run.' Team Stadium could stand back and be proud of their contribution to making the Games such a success. Together they had followed best practice at every stage of the project to build the best venue possible – a venue that met the needs of the Olympic athletes and those of the communities of the future.

This book has explained the seven principles of running a successful project, which together resulted in one of the most successful stadiums in modern Olympic history.

The seven principles of running a successful project

1   Have a common goal
2   Develop a detailed plan before you start
3   Develop a good communication strategy
4   Develop the ethos of good teamwork
5   Decide on the legacy from the outset
6   Develop robust checking procedures before you start
7   Make sure your project is fit for purpose

By applying these seven principles, Team Stadium was able to meet all the requirements of the demanding brief in design and construction by a delivery date that could not be moved.

1   They had a **common goal** and checked their progress against this goal on an ongoing basis. This meant that they stayed on track and avoided unnecessary work.

2   By having a **detailed plan** from the start, Team Stadium knew what they had to do and by when to meet the final deadline.

3 A good **communication strategy** helped Team Stadium provide the required information across the team on time to stay on track with the programme.

4 Team Stadium developed **good teamwork** early on, which meant that they could rely on each other to provide the right elements at the right time. They could test various ideas in an open and honest environment, which helped them achieve the overall goal by improving the final design and construction.

5 The fact that Team Stadium could **decide on the legacy** from the outset meant that this was at the front of everyone's mind during the whole design and construction process.

6 Team Stadium had **effective checking procedures** right from the start, which meant that any issues could be sorted out early, avoiding delays to the design and construction programme.

7 Finally, the team had the experience and technical ability to ensure that the design and construction of the stadium was **fit for purpose** and met all the requirements of the brief and the Olympic Authority.

This is not to say that Team Stadium discussed the seven principles before they started the project or were even aware that they were applying them throughout the project. Indeed, it is a testament to the team's wealth of experience and skill that following these seven principles was simply how they worked. Many of the things we do automatically are subconscious because we do them all the time, and at SSA the seven principles are inherent in what we do. But stripping back the way we work to identify them gives us a better understanding of the essential elements that make our business the success it is today.

I encourage new team members to embrace the seven principles. It is vital that they are confident to challenge, suggest new ways of working and offer new ideas. This is what breeds success and creates a good working environment for everyone. New members of the team are involved from the beginning of a project to give them a clear understanding of the client's requirements. To get other team members behind the project, the key is simply to have an open, honest discussion with them to explain and discuss the benefits of the various principles. The discussion could include ideas and comments from team members about how they could apply the seven principles to the project. This makes the team feel part of the process and buy into it.

We recruit people who believe in how we work. This builds team morale and buy-in and creates an environment of open, honest communication. It is now part of our interview process to explain to candidates how we work. We invite them to work for a full day with us so that we can see how they get on with the team. We believe that the success of our business is as much about personal relationships as it is about technical ability.

We have built our business on the seven principles set out in this book and they have had a great professional and financial impact. Professionally, we have developed a really good reputation in our local area – most of our work comes from referrals and recommendations. Financially, the company has grown to a healthy six-figure income in the last five years and turnover doubled in the last two years. We can't attribute all this to following the seven principles, but they are a fundamental part of it. You have to get your product right and out on time to satisfy the customer. If you have a satisfied customer, you will get repeat business and more referrals.

Creating a blueprint of the seven principles has helped us run successful projects more economically and with shorter programme times than would usually be the case. The principles allow us to allocate resources more cost-effectively and at the right time, as this has been planned from the start of the project.

The seven principles of running a successful project cover all construction projects and they apply to other sectors too. It has been proven time and again that applying these principles gives your project a far greater chance of success than if you did not apply them. They have a positive impact across the board, whether you are dealing with a large or small project.

There are undoubtedly other principles of running successful projects, but you will find that they are generally contained in the seven principles mentioned in this book.

No one principle takes priority – you can follow them in a different order and you might find that they overlap when you apply them. For example, you will put in place checking procedures throughout the life of the project, not just at the end.

Your communication strategy might start even as you are putting your team in place, especially if your project will affect the local community and you need to manage their expectations before the building starts. You should follow the seven principles concurrently and throughout the project.

How the seven principles benefit your business

As Benjamin Franklin said, 'failing to plan is planning to fail'. By including the seven principles in your project you will get the benefit of having a detailed plan from the start, which will give you more chance of success. You will change the way you approach your projects, which will give you a deeper understanding of your client's brief, their requirements and their true drivers for the project. This will give you more chance of success, professionally and financially.

You may even find that certain projects are not worth doing. By applying these principles, you will start to look at the nitty gritty of the project. As you dig deeper, you can see more clearly if a project is financially viable or not.

You will have confidence that you have covered all the important areas of the project, which will give you the greatest chance of success. Knowing that you have covered all the bases will also remove some of the stress and worry of running a project.

The client will benefit too, as their project will be well run, well thought out and properly detailed. It will be fit for purpose. You will improve the quality of what you do, saving time and money for your client. This will bring you financial success through repeat business and word-of-mouth referrals. You are only as good as your last project. At SSA we don't rest on our laurels – we want to be at our best always, showing our clients that we will give them the best solution and that we have their best interests at heart. The seven principles of running a successful project enable us to do that in a structured way.

A blueprint for the future

Team Stadium may have created a blueprint for future Olympic stadiums, in terms of their integrated model of working and embracing the temporary to meet legacy and sustainability goals. While some other Olympic stadiums had small elements of a temporary nature, the larger portion of the stadium in London was temporary, with only 25,000 permanent seats out of 80,000 seats. This needed a big mind shift in design and construction. The seven principles helped to make this change in thinking a success. The team had to do things differently and to do that, they needed a different way of working.

While this was not fully embraced for the 2016 Olympics, I hope that future Olympics will take heed of what was done in London in 2012 and make this part of their design where possible. By the 2020 and 2024 Olympics, designers will have had more time to go back and reflect on what was accomplished at London 2012 and incorporate the ideology of Team Stadium.

The contribution of London 2012

The London 2012 Olympic Games made a major and lasting contribution to improving the East End of London. The improvement begun by the Games has continued with the development of better shops, homes and transport in the area. With new skyscrapers and shopping centres, the area has been transformed from an industrial wasteland into a modern and thriving economic hub. This is all because of holding the Olympic Games there. The legacy of the Games for the East End is that they have brought the area into the twenty-first century.

The Olympic Park is the largest park created in Europe in recent years that has been left for local people to enjoy. The permanent venues (for example, the aquatic centre and the stadium) have provided world-class facilities for local people to use. These facilities will also be used to hold international swimming and athletics events. The London Olympics left behind good-quality, practical facilities that are all used all the time.

The success of Team Stadium's approach may have global implications for the Olympics in the longer term. If the London 2012 Olympic team had not made the sustainability and legacy ideals a reality, instead leaving London with buildings that would never be used again and decay, other countries might have been reluctant to bid for the Games. They might have believed that they could not afford to build stadiums to the required standard and that they would be left with a white elephant. Taking this to the extreme, this could spell the end of the Olympic Games because no country would be able to afford to host them.

The success of London 2012

Team Stadium provided stunning settings where athletes could give their best performances. During the course of the 2012 Olympics and Paralympic Games:

- 204 nations took part

- There were 47 gold-medal events for athletics in the London Olympic Games, where each of the Olympic champions were awarded a gold medal

- There were 166 gold-medal events for athletics in the Paralympics

- 32 world records were broken in 8 sports in the London Olympics, and

- 144 athletes broke world records in the Paralympics.

Keeping the Games clean

From the start, the organisers of London 2012 were determined to deal with the challenge posed by the threat of doping. Lord Coe, Chair of the London Organising Committee, declared the fight against drugs to be one of the underpinning principles of the bid that they made in 2005. A renowned anti-doping expert, Professor David Cowan, Head of the Department of Forensic Science at King's College London, was put in charge of the new state-of-the-art laboratory that would be used for the Games. The laboratory made it possible to analyse 6,000 urine samples and 1,000 blood samples taken from 10,500 athletes during the Games. These were tested by 160 staff at an average of 400 a day. Professor Cowan said that London would be 'the most tested games in history'. He added, 'We're helping to provide an Olympic Games that is as free from doping as is possible.'

This doping-control programme allowed more athletes to be tested than at any previous Games. Every competitor coming to London had a 50/50 chance of being tested, so any drugs cheats had a reasonable chance of being caught. The laboratory team tested as many athletes as they could to make London 2012 as clean as possible.

Summary

The seven principles of running a successful project provide a blueprint for success, regardless of the size of your project. By following these principles, you will be able to monitor the impact of how you work on the outcome of your project. For example, you may be able to complete a project earlier for your client because you have communicated more effectively across your team. Or you may find that your team have put forward ideas that have enabled you to do something differently and more cost-effectively for your client.

The seven principles will help your clients in many ways. Clients I have worked with say they prefer an open and honest approach. They like being given the facts in clear, non-technical language so they can understand what will happen and when. Clients will also receive a better product in a shorter time if you follow the seven principles. Following the principles can save your clients money too.

In conclusion, the seven principles of running a successful project give structure to what you do. Together, they provide a blueprint that results in:

- Benefits for your clients
- A better business reputation
- Repeat business
- More word-of-mouth referrals
- A higher income.

Finally, following this blueprint will give you a method to track your business success.

Why not apply the seven principles on your next project and monitor the effect this has on the project?

Look at the results.

Ask yourself:

- Did I deliver on time and within budget?

- Was the client happy with the communication my team provided throughout the project?

- Were they happy with the results?

- What feedback did my client give me?

Look at what you did differently this time. Think consciously about the seven principles and how you kept to them. If you are already following some of them unconsciously, this time stop and think about what you are doing at each step of the project and evaluate the impact on your project and programme.

Put simply, give it a go. You have nothing to lose and a lot to gain by applying the seven principles of running a successful project to your future work.

REFERENCES

The following sources were referred to during the writing of this book:

1   *The Architecture of London 2012* - Tom Dyckhoff and Claire Barrett.

2   *London 2012 Sustainable Design* - Hattie Hartman.

3   *London 2012 Olympics Stadium* - by HOK Sport.
    (https://www.dezeen.com/2007/11/07/london-2012-olympics-stadium-by-hok
    sport/)

4   *London Olympic Stadium News* - 21 July 2012. Interview with Phillip Johnson a
    principle architect at Populous.
    (https://www.e-architect.co.uk/london/london-olympic-stadium).

5   *London Olympic Stadium Building* - 21 December 2010 - Lights On.
    (https://www.e-architect.co.uk/london/london-olympic-stadium-construction).

6   London Stadium - Queen Elizabeth Olympic Park - Info on Opening Stadium.

7   *London 2012 - Olympic Stadium*. Peter Popp and Emilia Margaretha. Published
    08 June 2012 - DETAIL.
    (http://www.detail-online.com/article/london-2012-olympic-stadium-16402/).

8   London 2012: A different kind of Olympic Stadium - by Rod Sheard of Populous
(http://www.bbc.co.uk/news/uk-11418422).

9   *2012 Opening Ceremony* - Populous.
(http://populous.com/project/london-2012-olympic-stadium/).

10   *The Olympic Stadium, London*, by Populous. Building Architects Journal.
(https://www.architectsjournal.co.uk/home/the-olympic-stadium-london-by populous/8613538.article).

11   AJ Video: *London 2012; Video Olympic Stadium* by Architects Journal.
(https://architectureofthegames.net/2012-london/london-2012-video-olympic stadium-by-architects-journal/).

12   *London 2012 Olympic Stadium: Design and Construction* - Paul Westbury et al. The Structural Engineer V90 June 2012.

13   *Olympic Stadium, London* - Steel Construction Info.
(http://www.steelconstruction.info/Olympic_stadium_London).

14   *Steel Structure of the London 2012 Olympic Stadium*, by Graham Bizley.
(http://www.bdonline.co.uk/steel-structure-of-the-london-2012-olympic stadium/5016252.article).

15 *Best Practice Guidance for Hybrid Construction.* C.H. Goodchild and J. Glass - The Concrete Centre.

16 *Ipswich Town Football Club: the north stand* - Concrete Construction, April 2002, Pages 38 – 41.

17 *London 2012 Olympic and Paralympic Games* - The Official Commemorative Book. Tom Knight and Sybil Ruscoe.

18 *Olympics Cauldron – Opening and Closing Ceremonies.* (https://en.wikipedia.org/wiki/2012_Summer_Olympics_and_Paralympics cauldron).

19 *Olympic Stadium (London)* - Wikipedia. (https://en.wikipedia.org/wiki/Olympic_Stadium_(London).

20 *Procurement Methods for Olympics* - Master's Thesis, Dirk von Plessen (https://books.google.co.uk/books?id=z4iDAAAQBAJ&pg=PA66&lpg=PA66&dq=rhitects+Journal+London+2012+Olympic+Stadium+design&source=bl&ots=S7PMJaY01y&sig=Gm-PsrbH33biUixSpSX1W3ckdM&hl=en&sa=X&ed=0ahUKEwiU3sOz2KbTAhWhI8AKHR8-D9w4ChDoAQiMATAN#v=one page&q=Archit ects%20 Journal%20London%202012%20Olympic%2 Stadium%20design&f=false).

21 *2012 Forever Revisiting the London Olympics*. Magazine Features Building. (http://www.building.co.uk/2012-forever-revisiting-the-london-olympics/5082 880article).

22 *Opening and Closing Ceremony* - Olympic News. (https://www.olympic.org/news/london-2012-opening-and-closing-ceremony).

ACKNOWLEDGEMENTS

To my family, my wife Janet Mason, son Kent Mason and daughter Christa Mason, thank you for all your love, understanding and support throughout my career and particularly during the writing of this book, which meant that I was not around as much as I would have liked to have been.

To my departed parents James and Eileen Mason, for your love, support and instilling a good work ethic in me that has stood me in good stead throughout my life.

To my Godparents Liz and Edwin Jury, for your love, help, support and encouragement through the years for my career and all the big decisions in my life.

To my siblings and extended family, thank you for your support over the years.

To my beta test readers Stuart Holdsworth CEng BEng(Hons) MICE MIStructE, Bruno Postle BA(Hons) DipArch, Vanessa E J Lanham-Day, BSc(Hons) FCIM – Director of Communications Project Ltd, Stephen F Day – BSc(Hons) GMICE, MAPEA Director of Communications Project Ltd and Leslie J. Nicholls BSc, MCIOB – who undertook the near impossible task of making sense of my manuscript and providing me with such good feedback that improved the final version immensely.

To Daniel Priestley for helping me to decide on the title of the book *'Will it Stand Up?'* which helped bring it to life and made it real, and all those at Dent for encouraging me to take on this journey.

To Lucy McCarraher and Joe Gregory of Rethink Press for all their assistance, process and advice on bringing this book to fruition, without which, this book would not have seen the light of day.

To my KPI accountability group and all the others that have helped with my book in some way, you know who you are, so a big thank you for your help, advice and support.

To Rafal Kolodziej and Karol Michalowski for creating and amending the images used in this book, as your skills with Revit and computers are really impressive and have enhanced the images immensely.

Thank you to the London Legacy Development Corporation (LLDC) for giving me permission to write the book on the London 2012 Olympic Stadium.

To the Rt Hon Sir Vince Cable, my local MP, for your support and encouragement and words of advice in writing this book; this is really appreciated.

To all my colleagues and mentors that I have worked with over the last 30 plus years who have helped me develop as an engineer and as a person, both in Africa and here in the UK. Particular mention to Stuart Holdsworth CEng BEng(Hons) MICE MIStructE and John Cutlack Eur.Ing BSc(Eng) ACGI CEng MIStructE MCS, both of whom I met when I joined Jan Bobrowski & Partners in Twickenham in 2000. They guided me and helped me develop my experience in Sports and Leisure projects from racecourse stands, football stands to multi-purpose arenas such as the Centaur Building at Cheltenham Racecourse, which in turn enabled my dream of working on the London 2012 Olympic Stadium become a reality. Your support, guidance and belief in me helped me to become the successful structural engineer that I am today, so thank you for this and for your continued help, support and friendship.

Also to Ritchie Clapson CEng MIStructE, former MD of NRM Bobrowksi and Capita Bobrowski, who taught me some fundamental business lessons in running an engineering consultancy that I still use today for my own company and value your continued mentorship and advice when I need it as well as your ongoing friendship and interest in how my business is performing.

To Nigel Botterill and everyone at the Entrepreneur's Circle who has taught me about running a successful business. I have realised that while learning as much as you can is important, implementing what you learn is the most important ingredient to achieving notable success. The inspiration and support from you and my fellow members has been instrumental and I look forward to more in our journey together.

To the Richmond Chamber of Commerce, led by the CEO Anne Newton, for all your help, tuition and encouragement with growing my business over the last six years and for the awards that we have won over the years.

To all my staff, past and present, at Super Structures Associates: thank you for your support and hard work that has helped make the company so successful. I look forward to our continued joint success in the coming years.

THE AUTHOR

Derek Mason

Derek Mason CEng PrEng MSc(Eng) MSAICE MICE MIStructE is a Chartered Structural Engineer with over thirty years' experience in the field of structural engineering. He is also a registered Professional Engineer in South Africa and has worked on projects of various sizes and complexity in various parts of Africa, and has worked in the UK since 1998.

Derek has worked for a broad range of engineering consultants in South Africa and the UK, including Watermans, Capita Symonds as well as smaller niche consultants such as Jan Bobrowski & Partners and NRM Consultants. At Jan Bobrowski & Partners and NRM Bobrowski, Derek worked on a broad range of sports and leisure projects, including football and racecourse stands. NRM Bobrowski was sold to Capita Symonds in 2008, and Derek was involved with the London 2012 Olympic Stadium while working at both these firms.

Derek has had a passion for athletics, particularly the middle distances, since his secondary school days where he competed and set several records in the middle distances. He then moved to road races, including half marathons, and then onto full marathons. Derek has completed more than 100 full marathons, as well as 13 35-mile ultra-marathons in a running career that spans over 40 years.

Derek led the team that did the third-party check for the Structural Engineering and Technical Review of the London 2012 Olympic Stadium, working for the Olympic Delivery Authority (ODA). This covered both the structural engineering design checks as well as the on-site checking of the construction.

Derek is the founding Director of a multi-award-winning niche structural engineering consultancy, Super Structures Associates Limited. Derek has also been a consultant to Sky News on the collapse of a large crane into the Sao Paulo's Corinthians Arena in Brazil in November 2013, while it was being built for the FIFA Football World Cup held in June 2014.

You can find out more about Derek at:

www.superstructuresassociates.co.uk

https://www.linkedin.com/in/derek-mason-1628762b/?ppe=1

https://www.facebook.com/Superstructures-Associates-1374316006171873/

Derek can be contacted on: Derek.mason@ssaceltd.co.uk

Lightning Source UK Ltd.
Milton Keynes UK
UKOW07f1044071117

312314UK00001B/3/P